IMMORTALITY AND RESURRECTION

IMMORTALITY AND RESURRECTION

FOUR ESSAYS BY

*Oscar Cullmann, Harry A. Wolfson,
Werner Jaeger, and Henry J. Cadbury*

EDITED AND WITH AN INTRODUCTION BY

Krister Stendahl

The Macmillan Company
NEW YORK

Second Printing 1968

The Macmillan Company, New York

Library of Congress catalog card number:
65-17522

Printed in the United States of America

Acknowledgments

These four Ingersoll Lectures are here published with due permission as follows:

Professor Cullmann's lecture was published in book form by The Epworth Press, London (1958). Cf. also *The Harvard Divinity School Bulletin* 21 (1955/56), pp. 5-36; and below, p. 5, note 1.

Professor Wolfson's lecture was included in his *Religious Philosophy: A Group of Essays*, by the Belnap Press: Copyright 1961 by the President and Fellows of Harvard College. Cf. *The Harvard Divinity School Bulletin* 22 (1956/57), pp. 5-40.

Professor Jaeger's lecture was published in *The Harvard Theological Review* [Copyright 1959 by the President and Fellows of Harvard College] 52 (1959), pp. 135-47. It was included (in its English form) in the Second Edition of Jaeger's *Humanistische Reden und Vorträge*. (Berlin: Walter de Gruyter & Co., 1960), pp. 287-99.

Professor Cadbury's lecture was published in *The Harvard Theological Review* [Copyright 1960 by the President and Fellows of Harvard College] 53 (1960), pp. 1-26. It was included in The Miracles and the Resurrection (S.P.C.K. Theological Collections 3; London, 1964), pp. 79-94.

CONTENTS

BIOGRAPHICAL NOTES

Krister Stendahl is Frothingham Professor of Biblical Studies at Harvard University.

Oscar Cullmann is a Professor of the Theological Faculty of the University of Basel and of the Sorbonne.

Harry Austryn Wolfson is Nathan Littauer Professor of Hebrew Literature and Philosophy, Emeritus, at Harvard University.

Werner Jaeger was University Professor at Harvard at his death in 1961.

Henry Joel Cadbury is Hollis Professor of Divinity, Emeritus, at Harvard University.

INTRODUCTION

Krister Stendahl

THE INGERSOLL LECTURESHIP on "The Immortality of
Man" was established at Harvard University by a bequest of Caroline Haskell Ingersoll in 1894. She thereby
carried out the wishes of her father, George Goldthwait
Ingersoll.[1] The specificity of the topic considered in
these yearly lectures appears unusual in the history of
academic lectureships, and even more unusual in that
history is the fact that the lecturers—from the first,
George A. Gordon (1896) and William James (1897)
to the most recent, Jaroslav Pelikan (1963) and Amos
Wilder (1964)—have stuck faithfully to the assigned
topic. To be sure, there have been many facets to the
presentation, and there have been voices both *pro* and
con. Not only theology and philosophy have played
their parts. Shakespeare (George Herbert Palmer,
1912) and the Negro Spirituals (Howard Thurman,
1947) have furnished the texts; and various cultures
and faiths have been in focus: not only the Greeks
and the Romans (Benjamin I. Wheeler, 1898; Clifford
Herschel Moore, 1918) and Judaism (Louis Finkel-
stein, 1944), but also the Eskimos (Vilhjalmur Stef-

[1] George Goldthwait Ingersoll (1796–1863) was a Unitarian
minister, a graduate of Harvard College (1815) and of Harvard
Divinity School (1818). Harvard conferred on him the degree
of S.T.D. in 1845. The major part of his parish ministry was
carried out in Burlington, Vt. (1822–44). After a short time
in East Cambridge (1847–48) he settled in Keene, N.H. Some
of his sermons were published as tracts of the American Unitarian Association.

anson, 1952), Buddhism and Hinduism (William Sturgis Bigelow, 1909; Walter Eugene Clark, 1934), the Chinese (Shih Hu, 1945), and the American Indians (Clyde Klockhohn, 1948). This lectureship has over the years become the challenging opportunity to many philosophers and theologians, historians, anthropologists and linguists to formulate their views on immortality. In some cases they would perhaps not have done so ever, had it not been for the specificity of the Ingersoll bequest.

A sample—in addition to the names already mentioned—from the list of lectures indicates the width of the spectrum: Josiah Royce (1899), George Foot Moore (1914), Kirsopp Lake (1922), Edgar Sheffield Brightman (1925), Gustav Krüger (1926), Harry Emerson Fosdick (1927), Sir Robert Alexander Falconer (1930), Shailer Mathews (1933), Charles Harold Dodd (1935 and 1950), William Ernest Hocking (1936), George Lyman Kittredge (1937), Mikhail Ivanovich Rostovtzeff (1938), James Bissett Pratt (1940), Alfred North Whitehead (1941), Rufus M. Jones (1943), Georges Florovsky (1951), Willard Learoyd Sperry (1953), John Knox (1960), Hans Jonas (1961), and Paul Tillich (1962).[2] The fact that all the lecturers found it possible and meaningful to stay faithfully within the assigned topic of immortality is a strong indication of the persistent power of the idea of immortality in human life and thought.

[2] From 1896–1936 these lectures were published as separate titles (by Houghton, Mifflin & Co., in Boston [1896–1912]; by Harvard University Press [1914–35]; by Harper & Brothers [1936]). Since 1937 the lectures were published in *The Harvard Divinity School Bulletin*, except for a few which appeared in the *Harvard Theological Review* (the two by Jaeger and Cadbury here published, and the one by Hans Jonas).

The four lectures which constitute the present contribution to the discussion have, however, been chosen for an even more specific purpose. There is nothing new in the fact that the two concepts of immortality and resurrection stand in a certain tension to each other. Harry Wolfson's lecture traces some of the ways in which this tension was both recognized and overcome by the Church Fathers. But there is a new intensity to this tension in the minds of many modern students of religion. This tension—which makes it reasonable to deal with immortality and resurrection under the sign of an either/or rather than a both/and— is forcefully demonstrated in Oscar Cullmann's chapter with its stark contrast between Socrates and Jesus. It would be awkward for the Editor at this point to fancy himself as an arbitrator in the debate which is implicit and partly even explicit in the bringing together of these four chapters. But it may well be in order to place the discussion in the context of present-day scholarship.

The increased tension of which we speak is in many ways the mature fruit of radical historical criticism. Not only in the study of the Scriptures, but also in the study of Plato and of the highly honored representatives of the classical tradition, there was for centuries a "direct" approach. In these writings one found out how things really were or should be. Even in a great historian like Adolf von Harnack it is striking to find the real center of the Christian faith in what is reasonable and acceptable to his cultural and philosophical sentiment. His angry criticism of the *religionsgeschichtliche Schule*, and of Albert Schweitzer's picture of Jesus as a thoroughly first-century Jewish apocalypticist, can only be understood if one recognizes that Harnack was one of the last great exponents of this "direct" approach. Along such lines it remained almost impossible to allow for the fact that many of the views which Jesus and the apostles considered central to their faith were very different from those of, and even "unacceptable" to, the so-called modern man.

Barth's theology, Bultmann's *demythologizing*, John A. T. Robinson's *Honest to God* are all in their own ways answers to the recognition of historical scholarship that the world of ancient texts—including the Scriptures and those of the cherished worthies from Hellas—must be understood in their own terms before we ask the question about relevancy for later ages, our own included. A two-step approach is called for. First: What did a Jesus, or a Paul, or a Plato think that he thought? Second: What have their texts and the ideas contained in them come to mean to Western culture and what could they mean today? This distinction between an original meaning and later understandings has contributed greatly to our historical knowledge and fairness; it has made the problem of hermeneutics a crucial one in contemporary discussion.

One of the first models for thought and research, which emerged out of this new two-step approach when applied to scripture and theology, was the sharp distinction between "the Greek" and "the biblical" view. While this has led to substantial gains in clarification, it is now obvious that such a model requires many modifications. The "biblical" is not so much biblical as it is generally Semitic, far beyond the confines of "revelation"; or it is often just plain mythopoeic. And the "Greek" in this dichotomy is not the world of Homer or the Tragedians but that very special kind of Platonism and Stoicism which merged into the Hellenistic era (as Werner Jaeger's lecture clearly shows); or it is a catchword for Western philosophical sentiments. Furthermore, it must be noted that at no point in the history of the Christian tradition did the Church feel it to be its obligation to preserve the Semitic patterns of thought as distinct and superior to the Greek philosophical tradition. This sensitivity to "motifs" and "thought patterns" is a fruit of the historian's awareness of distance and his respect for the two-step approach of which we have spoken.

The studies of immortality and resurrection here presented make full sense only when seen in this general setting. They point toward—and they indicate the need for further clarification as to—the actual functions of the concepts of immortality and resurrection. They do not answer the question: What is the best way to think about these things? They furnish us with the building blocks for such thinking and they suggest how these blocks were used or rejected in the architectonic enterprises of times past. They give us the impression that the main "cathedrals" of Christian and Western thought were seldom completed in a purist style—whether the basilica of Immortality or the Gothic style of Resurrection. They suggest that both immortality and resurrection in their original settings are ideas which require creative interpretation and demythologizing if they are to fit into any pattern of twentieth-century thought. In that sense these chapters fit well into an era when immortality no longer has a deceptively attractive advantage over resurrection. To many of us, both concepts are equally suspect from the point of view of what is reasonable in accordance with common sense or experience. Once both concepts are recognized as mythological, there is a new possibility of assessing the role and significance and truth of such linguistic symbols.

If I am allowed to give the reader one suggestion as to what to look for, especially, when he reads these four chapters, I would urge him to make a chart—mentally, or actually on paper—of what function the two concepts here expounded have had or could have. By function I mean something very simple: What question(s) did or do the beliefs in immortality and resurrection answer? How do or did these concepts function in the minds and lives of men? Many modern readers take for granted that the belief in immortality is a source of consolation; or consider it a bulwark for the sacredness and absolute value of the individual. But it has often functioned as an equally obvious basis for the irrevocable necessity of purgatory and hell, or as a forceful reason for despising or downgrading all things temporal—from the human body to the realities of the body politic; or it has been considered a necessary presupposition for absolute ethical norms.

In the case of resurrection the different functions are even more diverse. The reader will find ample material for such observations in these chapters. He will come to recognize that the function of the resurrection of Jesus Christ was not primarily a reassurance to mankind that there is "resurrection" and hence eternal life. The Jews who first uttered or heard the message that Jesus was risen knew of and expected the resurrection, i.e., the general resurrection at the end of this age. To them the message meant—if accepted—that the last times had really dawned since the general resurrection had begun. Jesus was "the first-born from the dead." A great step into the "age to come" had been taken.

There is something astonishing and attractive in this

concern for God's promises to Israel and to the world, rather than for the self-centered question: What is going to happen to *my* soul? In its original setting the resurrection is an answer to *the* question of Judaism in the time of Jesus: the question of theodicy. Will justice win and God's promises to the faithful be fulfilled?

In that sense the resurrection was primarily an eschatological sign, an indication that the "new age" had dawned, that the last judgment was impending (Acts 17:31). It was the means by which Jesus was vindicated as the true Messiah. But it did not take long before the Easter message came to be applied as a spectacular answer to those concerns which expressed themselves in a hunger for eternal life, and to which the belief in immortality was *the* answer. And so the two concepts were welded together, as they had been already prior to the Christian movement. Especially among the Jews of the Diaspora, who were in close contact with the Hellenistic world, the stark language of resurrection was naturally related to the belief in immortality. When Josephus describes the tenets of both Essenes and Pharisees to the outside world, he speaks within the framework of the immortal and imperishable soul. The Pharisees, he says, consider "every soul imperishable, but only the soul of the good passes into another body, while those of the wicked suffer eternal punishment" (Jewish War II. viii. 14). Thus the immortality of the soul is a rational and necessary presupposition for a resurrection, and resurrection is the means by which the good are vindicated in the last judgment. When reporting the beliefs of the Essenes Josephus becomes even more explicit: "Emanating from the first ether, the souls become entangled, as it were, in the prison-house of the body, to which they are dragged down by a sort of natural spell; but when they are released from the bonds of the flesh, then, as though liberated from a long servitude, they rejoice and are borne aloft." Josephus goes on to point out that in these matters the Essenes shared the view of "the children of the Greeks," and he states that the aim of their teaching "was first to establish the doctrine of the immortality of the soul, and secondly to promote virtue and to deter from vice" (II. viii. 11).

I have chosen these specific examples to illustrate the problem of similarity and difference. Every reader of these passages from Josephus who is also familiar with the original statements of the Pharisees and the Essenes must ask himself to what extent this is not a drastically apologetic translation of their belief in the resurrection. Even if the Essene library found at Qumran (the Dead Sea Scrolls) does not contain explicit references to the resurrection (see Cadbury's lecture and the notes there given, below, p. 149), the tenor and context of those texts are far removed from the concerns epitomized by Josephus. The Qumran texts center around God's promised vindication of the elect, which we have seen to be the original matrix of the belief in the resurrection.

And so we could go on in our analysis of these two distinct strands of thought, which at many points in the history of Christianity and Judaism were fused and yet retained their mutual tension. It may seem to be the kind of tension which makes both Jewish and Christian reflection creatively uneasy within any thoroughly rational system of thought.

IMMORTALITY OF THE SOUL OR RESURRECTION OF THE DEAD

The Witness of the New Testament

THE INGERSOLL LECTURE FOR 1955

Oscar Cullmann

IF WE WERE to ask an ordinary Christian today (whether well-read Protestant or Catholic, or not) what he conceives to be the New Testament teaching concerning the fate of man after death, with few exceptions we should get the answer: "The immortality of the soul." Yet this widely accepted idea is one of the greatest misunderstandings of Christianity. There is no point in attempting to hide this fact, or to veil it by reinterpreting the Christian faith. This is something that should be discussed quite candidly. The concept of death and resurrection is anchored in the Christ-event (as will be shown in the following pages), and hence is incompatible with the Greek belief in immortality; because it is based in *Heilsgeschichte* it is offensive to modern thought. Is it not such an integral element of the early Christian proclamation that it can neither be surrendered nor reinterpreted without robbing the New Testament of its substance?[1]

[1] See on the following also O. Cullmann, "La foi à la résurrection et l'espérance de la résurrection dans le Nouveau Testament," *Etudes théol. et rel.* (1943), pp. 3ff.; *Christ and Time* (1945), pp. 231ff.; Ph. H. Menoud, *Le sort des trépassés* (1945); R. Mehl, *Der letzte Feind* (1954).

But is it really true that the early Christian resurrection faith is irreconcilable with the Greek concept of the immortality of the soul? Does not the New Testament, and above all the Gospel of John, teach that we already have eternal life? Is it really true that death in the New Testament is always conceived as "the last enemy" in a way that is diametrically opposed to Greek thought, which sees in death a friend? Does not Paul write: "O death, where is thy sting?" We shall see at the end that there *is* at least an analogy, but first we must stress the fundamental differences between the two points of view.

The widespread misunderstanding—that the New Testament teaches the immortality of the soul—was actually encouraged by the rocklike *post-Easter* conviction of the first disciples that the bodily resurrection of Christ had robbed death of all its horror[2] and that, from the moment of Easter onward, the Holy Spirit had awakened the souls of believers into the life of the resurrection.

The very fact that the words *"post-Easter"* need to be underlined illustrates the whole abyss which nevertheless separates the early Christian view from that of the Greeks. The whole of early Christian thought is based in *Heilsgeschichte*, and everything that is said about death and eternal life stands or falls with a belief in a real occurrence, in real events which took place in

---

[2] But hardly in such a way that the original Christian community could speak of "natural" dying. This manner of speaking of Karl Barth's in *Die kirchliche Dogmatik*, III, 2 (1948), pp. 776ff., though found in a section where otherwise the negative valuation of death as the "last enemy" is strongly emphasized, still seems to me not to be grounded in the New Testament. See I Cor. 11:30 (on that verse see below, pp. 32, 34).

time. This is the radical distinction from Greek thought. The purpose of my book *Christ and Time* was precisely to show that this belongs to the substance, to the essence of early Christian faith, that it is something not to be surrendered, not to be altered in meaning; yet it has often been mistakenly thought that I intended to write an essay on the New Testament attitude toward the problem of time and eternity.

If one recognizes that death and eternal life in the New Testament are always bound up with the Christ-event, then it becomes clear that for the first Christians the soul is not intrinsically immortal, but rather became so only through the resurrection of Jesus Christ, and through faith in him. It also becomes clear that death is not intrinsically the friend, but rather that its "sting," its power, is taken away *only* through the victory of Jesus over it in his death. And lastly, it becomes clear that the resurrection already accomplished is not the state of fulfillment, for that remains in the future until the body is also resurrected, which will not occur until "the last day."

It is a mistake to read into the Fourth Gospel an early trend toward the Greek teaching of immortality, because there also eternal life is bound up with the Christ-event.[3] Within the bounds of the Christ-event, of course, the various New Testament books place the accent in different places, but common to all is the view of *Heilsgeschichte*.[4] Obviously one must reckon with Greek influence upon the origin of Christianity from

[3] Insofar as John's Gospel is rooted in *Heilsgeschichte*, it is not true, as Rudolf Bultmann wrongly maintains, that a process of demythologizing is already to be discerned in it.

[4] As Bo Reicke correctly maintains, "Einheitlichkeit oder verschiedene Lehrbegriffe in der neutestamentlichen Theologie," *Theol. Zeitschr.*, 9 (1953), pp. 401ff.

the very beginning,[5] but so long as the Greek ideas are subordinated to the total view of *Heilsgeschichte*, there can be no talk of "Hellenization" in the proper sense.[6] Genuine Hellenization occurs for the first time at a later date.

I. THE LAST ENEMY: DEATH

Socrates and Jesus

NOTHING SHOWS more clearly than the contrast between the death of Socrates and that of Jesus (a contrast which was often cited, though for other purposes, by early opponents of Christianity) that the biblical view of death from the first is focused in salvation-history and so departs completely from the Greek conception.[7]

In Plato's impressive description of the death of Socrates, in the Phaedo, occurs perhaps the highest and most sublime doctrine ever presented on the immortality of the soul. What gives his argument its unex-

[5] All the more as the Qumran texts show that the Judaism to which embryonic Christianity was so closely connected was already itself influenced by Hellenism. See O. Cullmann, "The Significance of the Qumran Texts for Research into the Beginnings of Christianity," *Journ. of Bibl. Lit.*, 74 (1955), pp. 213ff.; also in K. Stendahl (ed.), *The Scrolls and the New Testament* (1957), pp. 18–32. So too Rudolf Bultmann, *Theology of the New Testament* (1955), Vol. II, p. 13 note.

[6] Rather, it would be more accurate to speak of a Christian "historicization" (in the sense of *Heilsgeschichte*) of the Greek ideas. Only in this sense, not in that employed by Bultmann, are the New Testament "myths" already "demythologized" by the New Testament itself.

[7] Material on this contrast in E. Benz, *Der gekreuzigte Gerechte bei Plato, im N.T., und in der alten Kirche* (1950).

celled value is his scientific reserve, his disclaimer of any proof having mathematical validity. We know the arguments he offers for the immortality of the soul: Our body is only an outer garment which, as long as we live, prevents our soul from moving freely and from living in conformity to its proper eternal essence. It imposes upon the soul a law which is not appropriate to it. The soul, confined within the body, belongs to the eternal world. As long as we live, our soul finds itself in a prison, that is, in a body essentially alien to it. Death, in fact, is the great liberator. It looses the chains, since it leads the soul out of the prison of the body and back to its eternal home. Since body and soul are radically different from one another and belong to different worlds, the destruction of the body cannot mean the destruction of the soul, any more than a musical composition can be destroyed when the instrument is destroyed.

Although the proofs of the immortality of the soul do not have for Socrates himself the same value as the proofs of a mathematical theorem, they nevertheless attain within their own sphere the highest possible degree of validity, and make immortality so probable that it amounts to a "fair chance" for man. And when the great Socrates traced the arguments for immortality in his address to his disciples on the day of his death, he did not merely *teach* this doctrine: at that moment he lived this doctrine. He showed how we serve the freedom of the soul, even in this present life, when we occupy ourselves with the eternal truths of philosophy. For through philosophy we penetrate into that eternal world of ideas to which the soul belongs, and we free the soul from the prison of the body. Death does no more than complete this liberation. Plato shows us how

Socrates goes to his death in complete peace and composure. The death of Socrates is a beautiful death. Nothing is seen here of death's terror. Socrates cannot fear death, since indeed it sets us free from the body. Whoever fears death proves that he loves the world of the body, that he is thoroughly entangled in the world of the senses. Death is the soul's great friend. So he teaches; and so, in wonderful harmony with his teaching, he dies—this man who embodied the Greek world in its noblest form.

And now let us hear how Jesus dies. In Gethsemane he knows that death stands before him, just as Socrates expected death on his last day. The synoptic evangelists furnish us, by and large, with a unanimous report. Jesus begins "to tremble and be distressed," writes Mark (14:33). "My soul is troubled, even to death," he says to his disciples.[8] Jesus is so thoroughly human that he shares the natural fear of death.[9] Jesus is afraid,

---

[8] Despite the parallel Jonah 4:9 which is cited by E. Klostermann, *Das Markus-Evangelium*, 3rd Edition (1936), ad loc., and E. Lohmeyer, *Das Evangelium des Markus* (1937), ad loc., I agree with J. Weiss, *Das Markus-Evangelium*, 3rd Edition (1917), ad loc., that the explanation: "I am so sad that I prefer to die" in this situation where Jesus *knows* that he is going to die (the scene is the Last Supper!) is completely unsatisfactory; moreover, Weiss's interpretation: "My affliction is so great that I am sinking under the weight of it" is supported by Mark 15:34. Also Luke 12:50, "How distressed I am until the baptism (=death) takes place," allows of no other explanation.

[9] Old and recent commentators (J. Wellhausen, *Das Evangelium Marci*, 2nd Edition (1909), ad loc., J. Schniewind in *Das N.T. Deutsch* (1934), ad loc., E. Lohmeyer, *Das Evangelium des Markus* (1937), ad loc., seek in vain to avoid this conclusion, which is supported by the strong Greek expressions for "tremble and shrink," by giving explanations which do not fit the situation, in which Jesus already knows that he must suffer for the sins of his people (Last Supper). In Luke 12:50 it is completely impossible to explain away the "distress" in the

though not as a coward would be of the men who will kill him, still less of the pain and grief which precede death. He is afraid in the face of death itself. Death for him is not something divine: it is something dreadful. Jesus does not want to be alone in this moment. He knows, of course, that the Father stands by to help him. He looks to him in this decisive moment as he has done throughout his life. He turns to God with all his human fear of this great enemy, death. He is afraid of death. It is useless to try to explain away Jesus' fear as reported by the evangelists. The opponents of Christianity who already in the first centuries made the contrast between the death of Socrates and the death of Jesus saw more clearly here than the exponents of Christianity. He was really afraid. Here is nothing of the composure of Socrates, who met death peacefully as a friend. To be sure, Jesus already knows the task which has been given him: to suffer death; and he has already spoken the words: "I have a baptism with which I must be baptized, and *how distressed* (or *afraid*) *I am* until it is accomplished" (Luke 12:50). Now, when God's enemy stands before him, he cries to God, whose omnipotence he knows: "All things are possible with thee; let this cup pass from me" (Mark 14:36). And when he concludes, "Yet not as I will, but as thou wilt," this does not mean that at the last he, like Socrates, regards death as the friend, the liberator. No, he means only this: If this greatest of all terrors, death, must befall me according to thy will,

---

face of death, and also in view of the fact that Jesus is abandoned by God on the cross (Mark 15:34), it is not possible to explain the Gethsemane scene except through this distress at the prospect of being abandoned by God, an abandonment which will be the work of death, God's great enemy.

then I submit to this horror. Jesus knows that in itself, because death is the enemy of God, to die means to be utterly forsaken. Therefore he cries to God; in the face of this enemy of God he does not want to be alone. He wants to remain as closely tied to God as he has been throughout his whole earthly life. For whoever is in the hands of death is no longer in the hands of God, but in the hands of God's enemy. At this moment, Jesus seeks the assistance, not only of God, but even of his disciples. Again and again he interrupts his prayer and goes to his most intimate disciples, who are trying to fight off sleep in order to be awake when the men come to arrest their master. They try; but they do not succeed, and Jesus must wake them again and again. Why does he want them to keep awake? He does not want to be alone. When the terrible enemy, death, approaches, he does not want to be forsaken even by the disciples whose human weakness he knows. "Could you not watch one hour?" (Mark 14:37).

Can there be a greater contrast than that between Socrates and Jesus? Like Jesus, Socrates has his disciples about him on the day of his death; but he discourses serenely with them on immortality. Jesus, a few hours before his death, trembles and begs his disciples not to leave him alone. The author of the epistle to the Hebrews, who, more than any other New Testament author, emphasizes the full deity (1:10) but also the full humanity of Jesus, goes still further than the reports of the three Synoptists in his description of Jesus' fear of death. In 5:7 he writes that Jesus "with loud cries and tears offered up prayers and supplications to him who was able to save him."[10] Thus, according

---

[10] The reference to Gethsemane here seems to me unmistakable. J. Héring, *L'Epître aux Hébreux* (1954), ad loc., concurs in this.

to the epistle to the Hebrews, Jesus wept and cried in the face of death. There is Socrates, calmly and composedly speaking of the immortality of the soul; here Jesus, weeping and crying.

And then the death-scene itself. With sublime calm Socrates drinks the hemlock; but Jesus, thus says the evangelist Mark (15:34)—we dare not gloss it over, cries: "My God, my God, why hast thou forsaken me?" And with another inarticulate cry he dies (Mark 15:37). This is not "death as a friend." This is death in all its frightful horror. This is really *the last enemy* of God. This is the name Paul gives it in I Corinthians 15:26, where the whole contrast between Greek thought and Christianity is disclosed.[11] Using different words, the author of the Johannine Apocalypse also regards death as the last enemy, when he describes how at the end death will be cast into the lake of fire (Rev. 20:14). Because it is God's enemy, it separates us from God, who is life and the creator of all life. Jesus, who is so closely tied to God, tied as no other man has ever been, for precisely this reason must experience death much more terribly than any other man. To be in the hands of the great enemy of God means to be forsaken by God. In a way quite different from others, Jesus must suffer this abandonment, this separation from God, the only condition really to be feared. Therefore he cries to God: "Why hast thou forsaken me?" He is now actually in the hands of God's great enemy.

[11] The problem is presented in entirely false perspective by J. Leipoldt, *Der Tod bei Griechen und Juden* (1942). To be sure, he correctly makes a sharp distinction between the Greek view of death and the Jewish. But Leipoldt's efforts always to equate the Christian with the Greek and oppose it to the Jewish only become comprehensible when one notes the year in which this book was published and the series (*Germanentum, Christentum und Judentum*) of which it is a part.

We must be grateful to the evangelists for having glossed over nothing at this point. Later (as early as the beginning of the second century, and probably even earlier) there were people who took offense at this—people of Greek provenance. In early Christian history we call them Gnostics.

I have put the death of Socrates and the death of Jesus side by side. For nothing shows better the radical difference between the Greek doctrine of the immortality of the soul and the Christian doctrine of the resurrection. Because Jesus underwent death in all its horror, not only in his body, but also in his soul ("My God, why hast thou forsaken me"), and as he is regarded by the first Christians as the mediator of salvation, he must indeed be the very one who in his death conquers death itself. He cannot obtain this victory by simply living on as an immortal soul, thus fundamentally *not* dying. He can conquer death only by actually dying, by betaking himself to the sphere of death, the destroyer of life, to the sphere of "nothingness," of abandonment by God. When one wishes to overcome someone else, one must enter his territory. Whoever wants to conquer death must die; he must really cease to live—not simply live on as an immortal soul, but die in body and soul, lose life itself, the most precious good which God has given us. For this reason the evangelists, who nonetheless intended to present Jesus as the Son of God, have not tried to soften the terribleness of his thoroughly human death.

Furthermore, if life is to issue out of so genuine a death as this, a new divine act of creation is necessary. And this act of creation calls back to life not just a part of the man, but the whole man—all that God had created and death had annihilated. For Socrates and

Plato no new act of creation is necessary. For the body is indeed bad and should not live on. And that part which is to live on, the soul, does not die at all.

If we want to understand the Christian faith in the resurrection, we must completely disregard the Greek thought that the material, the bodily, the corporeal is bad and *must* be destroyed, so that the death of the body would not be in any sense a destruction of the true life. For Christian (and Jewish) thinking, the death of the body is *also* destruction of God-created life. No distinction is made: even the life of our body is true life; death is the destruction of *all* life created by God. Therefore it is death and not the body which must be conquered by the resurrection.

Only he who apprehends with the first Christians the horror of death, who takes death seriously as death, can comprehend the Easter exultation of the primitive Christian community and understand that the whole thinking of the New Testament is governed by belief in the resurrection. Belief in the immortality of the soul is not belief in a revolutionary event. Immortality, in fact, is only a *negative* assertion: the soul does *not* die, but simply lives on. Resurrection is a *positive* assertion: the whole man, who has really died, is recalled to life by a new act of creation by God. Something has happened—a miracle of creation! For something has also happened previously, something fearful: life formed by God has been destroyed.

Death in itself is not beautiful, not even the death of Jesus. Death before Easter is really the death's head surrounded by the odor of decay. And the death of Jesus is as loathsome as the great painter Grünewald depicted it in the Middle Ages. But precisely for this reason the same painter understood how to paint, along with it, in an incomparable way, the great victory, the resurrection of Christ: Christ in the new body, the resurrection body. Whoever paints a pretty death can paint no resurrection. Whoever has not grasped the horror of death cannot join Paul in the hymn of victory: "Death is swallowed up—in victory! O death, where is thy victory? O death, where is thy sting?" (I Cor. 15:54f.).

II. THE WAGES OF SIN: DEATH

Body and Soul—Flesh and Spirit

YET THE contrast between the Greek idea of the immortality of the soul and the Christian belief in the resurrection is still deeper. The belief in the resurrection presupposes the Jewish connection between death and *sin*. Death is not something natural, willed by God, as in the thought of the Greek philosophers; it is rather something unnatural, abnormal, opposed to God.[12] The Genesis narrative teaches us that it came into the world only by the sin of man. Death is a curse, and the whole creation has become involved in the curse. The sin of man has necessitated the whole series of events which the Bible records and which we call the story of redemption. Death can be conquered only to the extent that sin is removed. For "death is the wages of sin." It is not only the Genesis narrative which speaks thus. Paul says the same thing (Rom. 6:23),

---

[12] We shall see that death, in view of its conquest by Christ, has lost all its horror. But I still would not venture as does Karl Barth, *Die kirchliche Dogmatik*, III, 2 (1948), pp. 777ff. (on the basis of the "second death" distinguished in Rev. 21:8), to speak in the name of the New Testament of a "natural death" (see I Cor. 11:30!).

and this is the view of death held by the whole of primitive Christianity. Just as sin is something opposed to God, so is its consequence, death. To be sure, God can make use of death (I Cor. 15:35ff., John 12:24), as he can make use of Satan to man.

Nevertheless, death *as such* is the enemy of God. For God is life and the creator of life. It is not by the will of God that there are withering and decay, dying and sickness, the by-products of death working in our life. All these things, according to Christian and Jewish thinking, come from human sin. Therefore, every healing which Jesus accomplishes is not only a driving back of death, but also an invasion of the province of sin; and therefore on every occasion Jesus says: "Your sins are forgiven." Not as though there were a corresponding sin for every individual sickness; but rather, like the presence of death, the fact that sickness exists at all is a consequence of the sinful condition of the whole of humanity. Every healing is a partial resurrection, a partial victory of life over death. That is the Christian point of view. According to the Greek interpretation, on the contrary, bodily sickness is a corollary of the fact that the body is bad in itself and is ordained to destruction. For the Christian an anticipation of the resurrection can already become visible, even in the earthly body.

That reminds us that the body is in no sense bad in itself, but is, like the soul, a gift of our creator. Therefore, according to Paul, we have duties with regard to our body. God is the *creator* of all things. The Greek doctrine of immortality and the Christian hope in the resurrection differ so radically because Greek thought has such an entirely different interpretation of creation. The Jewish and Christian interpretation of creation excludes the whole Greek dualism of body and soul. For indeed the visible, the corporeal, is just as truly God's creation as the invisible. God is the maker of the body. The body is not the soul's prison, but rather a temple, as Paul says (I Cor. 6:19): the temple of the Holy Spirit! The basic distinction lies here. Body and soul are not opposites. God finds the corporeal "good" after he has created it. The Genesis story makes this emphasis explicit. Conversely, moreover, sin also embraces the whole man, not only the body, but the soul as well; and its consequence, death, extends over all the rest of creation. Death is accordingly something dreadful, because the whole visible creation, including our body, is something wonderful, even if it is corrupted by sin and death. Behind the pessimistic interpretation of death stands the optimistic view of creation. Wherever, as in Platonism, death is thought of in terms of liberation, there the visible world is not recognized directly as God's creation.

Now, it must be granted that in Greek thought there is also a very positive appreciation of the body. But in Plato the good and beautiful in the corporeal are not good and beautiful in virtue of corporeality but rather, so to speak, *in spite of* corporeality: the soul, the eternal and the only substantial reality of being, shines faintly through the material. The corporeal is not the real, the eternal, the divine. It is merely that through which the real appears—and then only in debased form. The corporeal is meant to lead us to contemplate the pure archetype, freed from all corporeality, the invisible idea.

To be sure, the Jewish and Christian points of view also see something else besides corporeality. For the whole creation is corrupted by sin and death. The creation which we see is not as God willed it, as he created it; nor is the body which we wear. Death rules over all; and it is not necessary for annihilation to accomplish its work of destruction before this fact becomes apparent—it is already obvious in the whole outward form of all things. Everything, even the most beautiful, is marked by death. Thus it might seem as if the distinction between Greek and Christian interpretation is not so great after all. And yet it remains radical. Behind the corporeal appearance Plato senses the incorporeal, transcendent, pure idea. Behind the corrupted creation, under sentence of death, the Christian sees the future creation brought into being by the resurrection, just as God willed it. The contrast, for the Christian, is not between the body and the soul, not between outward form and idea, but rather between the creation delivered over to death by sin and new creation; between the corruptible, fleshly body and the incorruptible resurrection body.

This leads us to a further point: the Christian interpretation of man. The anthropology of the New Testament is not Greek, but is connected with Jewish conceptions. For the concepts of body, soul, flesh, and spirit (to name only these), the New Testament does indeed use the same words as the Greek philosopher. But they mean something quite different; and we understand the whole New Testament amiss when we construe these concepts only from the point of view of Greek thought. Many misunderstandings arise thus. I cannot present here a biblical anthropology in detail. There are good monographs on the subject,[13] not to mention the appropriate articles in Kittel's *Theolo-*

[13] W. G. Kümmel, *Das Bild des Menschen im Neuen Testament* (1948).

gisches Wörterbuch. A complete study would have to treat separately the anthropologies of the various New Testament authors, since on this point there exist differences which are by no means unimportant.[14] Of necessity I can deal here only with a few cardinal points which concern our problem, and even this must be done somewhat schematically, without taking into account the nuances which would have to be discussed in a proper anthropology. In so doing, we shall naturally have to rely primarily upon Paul, since only in his writings do we find an anthropology which is definable in detail, even though he too fails to use the different ideas with complete consistency.[15]

The New Testament certainly knows the difference between body and soul, or more precisely, between the inner and the outer man. This distinction does not, however, imply opposition, as if the one were by nature good, the other by nature bad.[16] Both belong together, both are created by God. The inner man without the outer has no proper, full existence. It requires a body. It can, to be sure, somehow lead a shady existence without the body, like the dead in Sheol according to the Old Testament, but that is not a *genuine life.* The

[14] Also the various theologies of the New Testament should here be mentioned.

[15] W. Cutbrod, *Die paulinische Anthropologie* (1934); W. G. Kümmel, *Römer 7 und die Bekehrung des Paulus* (1929); E. Schweizer, "Röm. 1:3f. und der Gegensatz von Fleisch und Geist vor und bei Paulus," *Evang. Theol.,* 15 (1955), pp. 563ff.; and especially the relevant chapter in R. Bultmann, *Theology of the New Testament* (1955).

[16] Also the words of Jesus in Mark 8:36, Matt. 6:25 and 10:28 ($\psi v\chi \acute{\eta}$ = life) do not speak of an "infinite value of the immortal soul" and presuppose no higher valuation of the inner man. See also (also *re* Mark 14:38) Kümmel, *Das Bild des Menschen,* pp. 16ff.

contrast with the Greek soul is clear: it is precisely apart from the body that the Greek soul attains to full development of its life. According to the Christian view, however, it is the inner man's very nature which demands the body.

And what now is the role played by the flesh ($\sigma \acute{\alpha} \rho \xi$) and spirit ($\pi \nu \epsilon \hat{\upsilon} \mu \alpha$)? Here it is especially important not to be misled by the secular use of the Greek words, though it is found in various places even in the New Testament and even within individual writers whose use of terminology is never completely uniform. With these reservations, we may say that according to the use which is characteristic, say, for Pauline theology, flesh and spirit in the New Testament are two *transcendent* powers which can enter into man from without; but *neither is given with human existence as such*. On the whole it is true that the Pauline anthropology, contrary to the Greek, is grounded in *Heilsgeschichte*.[17] "Flesh" is the power of sin or the power of death. It seizes the outer and the inner man *together*. *Spirit* ($\pi \nu \epsilon \hat{\upsilon} \mu \alpha$) is its great antagonist: the power of creation. It also seizes the outer and inner man *together*. Flesh and spirit are active powers, and as such they work within us. The flesh, the power of death, entered man with the sin of Adam; indeed it entered the whole man, inner and outer; yet in such a way that it is very closely linked with the body. The inner man finds itself less closely connected with the flesh;[18] although through

---

[17] This is what Kümmel means when he states that in the New Testament, including the Johannine theology, man is always conceived as an *historical* being.

[18] The body is, so to speak, its locus, from which point it affects the whole man. This explains why Paul is able to speak of "body" instead of "flesh," or conversely "flesh" instead of "body," contrary to his own basic conception, although this

guilt this power of death has more and more taken possession even of the inner man. The spirit, on the other hand, is the great power of life, the element of the resurrection; God's power of creation is given to us through the Holy Spirit. In the Old Testament the spirit is at work only from time to time in the prophets. In the end-time in which we live—that is, since Christ has broken the power of death in his own death and has arisen—this power of life is at work in all members of the community (Acts 2:17: "in the last days"). Like the flesh, it too already takes possession of the whole man, inner and outer. But whereas, in this age, the flesh has established itself to a substantial degree in the body, though it does not rule the inner man in the same inescapable way, the quickening power of the Holy Spirit is already taking possession of the inner man so decisively that the inner man is "renewed from day to day," as Paul says (II Cor. 4:16). The whole Johannine Gospel emphasizes the point. We are already in the state of resurrection, that of eternal life— not immortality of soul: the new era is already inaugurated. The body, too, is already in the power of the Holy Spirit.

Wherever the Holy Spirit is at work we have what amounts to a momentary retreat of the power of death, a certain foretaste of the end.[19] This is true even in the body, hence the healings of the sick. But here it is a question only of a retreat, not of a final transformation of the body of death into a resurrection body. Even

---

occurs in very few passages. These terminological exceptions do not alter his general view, which is characterized by a sharp distinction between body and flesh.

[19] See my article, "La délivrance anticipée du corps humain d'après le Nouveau Testament," *Hommage et Reconnaissance. 60° anniversaire de K. Barth* (1946), pp. 31ff.

those whom Jesus raised up in his lifetime will die again, for they did not receive a resurrection body, the transformation of the fleshly body into a spiritual body does not take place until the end. Only then will the Holy Spirit's power of resurrection take such complete possession of the body that it transforms it in the way it is already transforming the inner man. It is important to see how different the New Testament anthropology is from that of the Greeks. Body and soul are both originally good insofar as they are created by God; they are both bad insofar as the deadly power of the flesh has hold of them. Both can and must be set free by the quickening power of the Holy Spirit.

Here, therefore, deliverance consists not in a release of soul from body but in a release of both from flesh. We are not released from the body; rather the body itself is set free. This is made especially clear in the Pauline epistles, but it is the interpretation of the whole New Testament. In this connection one does not find the differences which are present among the various books on other points. Even the much-quoted saying of Jesus in Matt. 10:28 in no way presupposes the Greek conception. "Fear not them that kill the body, but cannot kill the soul." It might seem to presuppose the view that the soul has no need of the body, but the context of the passage shows that this is not the case. Jesus does not continue: "Be afraid of him who kills the soul"; rather: "Fear him who can slay both soul *and* body in Gehenna." That is, fear God, who is able to give you over completely to death; to wit, when he does not resurrect you to life. We shall see, it is true, that the soul is the starting-point of the resurrection, since, as we have said, it can already be possessed by the Holy Spirit in a way quite different from the body. The Holy Spirit already lives in our inner man. "By the Holy Spirit who dwells in you (already)," says Paul in Rom. 8:11, "God will also quicken your mortal bodies." Therefore, those who kill only the body are not to be feared. It can be raised from the dead. Moreover, it must be raised. The soul cannot always remain without a body. And on the other side we hear in Jesus' saying in Matt. 10:28 that the soul can be killed. The soul is not immortal. There must be resurrection for both; for since the Fall the whole man is "sown corruptible." For the inner man, thanks to the transformation by the quickening power of the Holy Spirit, the resurrection can take place already in this present life: through the "renewal from day to day." The flesh, however, still maintains its seat in our body. The transformation of the body does not take place until the end, when the whole creation will be made new by the Holy Spirit, when there will be no death and no corruption.

The resurrection of the body, whose substance[20] will no longer be that of the flesh, but that of the Holy Spirit, is only a part of the *whole new creation*. "We wait for a new heaven *and* a new earth," says II Pet. 3:13. The Christian hope relates not only to my individual fate, but to the entire creation. Through sin the whole creation has become involved in death. This we hear not only in Genesis, but also in Rom. 8:19ff., where Paul writes that the whole creation[21] from now on waits longingly for deliverance. This deliverance

[20] I use this rather unfortunate term for want of a better. What I mean by it will be clear from the preceding discussion.

[21] The allusion in verse 20 to the words "for your sake" of Genesis 3:17 excludes the translation of κτίσις as "creature" in the sense of man, a translation advocated by E. Brunner and A. Schlatter. See O. Cullmann, *Christ and Time* (1950), p. 103.

will come when the power of the Holy Spirit transforms all matter, when God in a new act of creation
will not *destroy* matter, but set it free from the flesh,
from corruptibility. Not eternal ideas, but concrete
objects will then rise anew, in the new, incorruptible
life-substance of the Holy Spirit; and among these
objects belongs our body as well.

Because resurrection of the body is a new act of
creation which embraces everything, it is not an event
which begins with each individual death, but only at
the *end*. It is not a transition from this world to
another world, as is the case of the immortal soul freed
from the body; rather it is the transition from the
present age to the future. It is tied to the whole
process of redemption.

Because there is sin, there must be a process of
redemption enacted in time. Where sin is regarded as
the source of death's lordship over God's creation,
there this sin and death must be vanquished together,
and there the Holy Spirit, the only power able to
conquer death, must win all creatures back to life in a
continuous process.

Therefore the Christian belief in the resurrection, as
distinct from the Greek belief in immortality, is tied
to a *divine total process* implying deliverance. Sin and
death must be conquered. We cannot do this. *Another*
has done it for us; and he was able to do it only in
that he betook himself to the province of death—that
is, he himself died and expiated sin, so that death as
the wages of sin is overcome. Christian faith proclaims
that Jesus has done this and that he arose *with* body
and soul after he was fully and really dead. Here God
has consummated the miracle of the new creation
expected at the end. Once again he has created life

as in the beginning. At this one point, in Jesus Christ, this has already happened! Resurrection, not only in the sense of the Holy Spirit's taking possession of the *inner* man, but also resurrection of the *body*. This is a new creation of matter—an incorruptible matter. Nowhere else in the world is there this new spiritual matter. Nowhere else is there a spiritual body—only here in Christ.

III. THE FIRST-BORN FROM THE DEAD

Between the Resurrection of Christ and the Destruction of Death

WE MUST take into account what it meant for the Christians when they proclaimed: Christ is risen from the dead! Above all we must bear in mind what death meant for them. We are tempted to associate these powerful affirmations with the Greek thought of the immortality of the soul, and in this way to rob them of their content. Christ is risen: that is, we stand in the new era in which death is conquered, in which corruptibility is no more. For if there is really *one* spiritual body (not an immortal soul, but a spiritual body) which has emerged from a fleshly body, then indeed the power of death is broken. Believers, according to the conviction of the first Christians, would no longer die: this was certainly their expectation in the earliest days. It must have been a problem when they discovered that Christians continued to die. But even the fact that men continue to die no longer has the same significance after the resurrection of Christ. The fact of death is robbed of its former significance. Dying is no longer an expression of the absolute lordship of death, but only one of death's last contentions for lordship. Death cannot put an end to the great fact that there is *one* risen body.

We ought to try simply to understand what the first Christians meant when they spoke of Christ as being the "first-born from the dead." However difficult it may be for us to do so, we must exclude the question whether or not we can accept this belief. We must also at the very start leave on one side the question whether Socrates or the New Testament is right. Otherwise we shall find ourselves continually mixing alien thought-processes with those of the New Testament. We should for once simply listen to what the New Testament says. Christ the first-born from the dead! His body the first resurrection body, the first spiritual body. Where this conviction is present, the whole of life and the whole of thought must be influenced by it. The whole thought of the New Testament remains for us a book sealed with seven seals if we do not read behind every sentence there this other sentence: Death has already been overcome (death, be it noted, not the body); there is already a new creation (a new creation, be it noted), not an immortality which the soul has always possessed) the resurrection age is already inaugurated.[22]

Granted that it is only inaugurated, but still it is

[22] If, as the Qumran fragment [4 Q Florileqium i.8; see A. Dupont-Sommer, *The Essene Writings from Qumran* (Meridian Books, 1962), p. 312] seems to confirm, the "teacher of righteousness" of this sect really was put to death and his return was awaited, still what most decisively separates this sect from the original Christian community (apart from the other differences, for which see my article previously referred to in note 5, p. 12) is the absence in it of faith in a resurrection which has *already* occurred.

decisively inaugurated. *Only* inaugurated: for death is at work, and Christians still die. The disciples experienced this as the first members of the Christian community died. This necessarily presented them with a difficult problem.[23] In I Cor. 11:30 Paul indicates that basically death and sickness should no longer occur. We still die, and still there is sickness and sin. But the Holy Spirit is already effective in our world as the power of new creation; he is already at work visibly in the primitive community in the diverse manifestations of the Spirit. In my book *Christ and Time* I have spoken of a tension between present and future, the tension between "already fulfilled" and "not yet consummated." This tension belongs *essentially* to the New Testament and is not introduced as a secondary solution born of embarrassment,[24] as Albert Schweitzer's disciples and Rudolf Bultmann maintain.[25] This tension is already present in and with Jesus. He proclaims the Kingdom of God for the future; but on the other hand, he proclaims that the Kingdom of God has already broken in, since he himself with the Holy Spirit is indeed already repulsing death by healing the sick and raising the dead (Matt. 12:28, 11:3ff., Luke 10:18) in anticipation of the victory over death which he obtains in his own death. Schweitzer is not right

[23] See in this regard Ph. H. Menoud, "La mort d'Ananias et de Saphira," *Aux sources de la tradition chrétienne. Mélanges offerts à M. Goguel* (1950), particularly pp. 150ff.

[24] See particularly F. Buri, "Das Problem der ausgebliebenen Parusie," *Schweiz. Theol. Umschau* (1946), pp. 97ff. See in addition O. Cullmann, "Das wahre durch die ausgebliebene Parusie gestillte neutestamentliche Problem," *Theol. Zeitschr.*, 3 (1947), pp. 177ff.; also pp. 428ff.

[25] R. Bultmann, "History and Eschatology in the New Testament," *New Test. Stud.*, 1 (1954), pp. 5ff.

when he sees as the original Christian hope *only* a hope in the future; nor is C. H. Dodd when he speaks *only* of realized eschatology; still less Bultmann when he resolves the original hope of Jesus and the first Christians into existentialism. It belongs to the very stuff of the New Testament that it thinks in temporal categories, and this is because the belief that in Christ the resurrection is achieved is the starting-point of all Christian living and thinking. When one starts from this principle, then the chronological tension between "already fulfilled" and "not yet consummated" constitutes the *essence* of the Christian faith. Then the metaphor I use in *Christ and Time* characterizes the whole New Testament situation: the decisive battle has been fought in Christ's death and resurrection; only V-day is yet to come.

Basically the whole contemporary theological discussion turns upon this question: Is *Easter* the starting-point of the Christian Church, of its existence, life, and thought? If so, we are living in an interim time.

In that case, the faith in resurrection of the New Testament becomes the cardinal point of all Christian belief. Accordingly, the fact that there is a resurrection body—Christ's body—defines the first Christians' whole interpretation of time. If Christ is the "first-born from the dead," then this means that the end-time is already present. But it also means that a temporal interval separates the first-born from all other men who are not yet "born from the dead." This means then that we live in an interim time, between Jesus' resurrection, which has already taken place, and our own, which will not take place until the end. It also means, moreover, that the quickening power, the Holy Spirit,

is already at work among us. Therefore Paul designates
the Holy Spirit by the same term—ἀπαρχή, firstfruits
(Rom. 8:23)—as he uses for Jesus himself (I Cor.
15:23). There is then already a foretaste of the resurrection. And indeed in a twofold way: our inner man is
already being renewed from day to day by the Holy
Spirit (II Cor. 4:16; Eph. 3:16); the body also has
already been laid hold of by the Spirit, although the
flesh still has its citadel within it. Wherever the Holy
Spirit appears, the vanquished power of death recoils,
even in the body. Hence miracles of healing occur even
in our still mortal body. To the despairing cry in Rom.
7:24, "Who shall deliver me from this body of death?"
the whole New Testament answers: the Holy Spirit!

The foretaste of the end, realized through the Holy
Spirit, becomes most clearly visible in the early Christian celebration of the breaking of bread. Visible miracles of the Spirit occur there. There the Spirit tries to
break through the limits of imperfect human language
in the speaking with tongues. And there the community passes over into direct connection with the
Risen One, not only with his soul, but also with his
resurrection body. Therefore we hear in I Cor. 10:16:
"The bread we break, is it not communion with the
body of Christ?" Here in communion with the brethren
we come nearest to the resurrection body of Christ;
and so Paul writes in the following chapter (a passage
which has received far too little consideration): if this
Lord's Supper were partaken of by all members of the
community in a completely worthy manner, then the
union with Jesus' resurrection body would be so effective in our own bodies that even now there would be
no more sickness or death (I Cor. 11:28–30)—a singu-

larly bold assertion.[26] Therefore the community is described as the body of Christ, because here the spiritual body of Christ is present, because here we come closest to it; here in the common meal the first disciples at Easter saw Jesus' resurrection body, his spiritual body.

Yet in spite of the fact that the Holy Spirit is already so powerfully at work, men still die; even after Easter and Pentecost men continue to die as before. Our body remains mortal and subject to sickness. Its transformation into the spiritual body does not take place until the whole creation is formed anew by God. Then only, for the first time, there will be nothing but Spirit, nothing but the power of life, for then death will be destroyed with finality. Then there will be a new substance for all things visible. Instead of the fleshly matter there appears the spiritual. That is, *instead of corruptible matter there appears the incorruptible.* The visible and the invisible will be spirit. But let us make no mistake: this is certainly not the Greek sense of bodiless Idea! A new heaven *and* a new earth! That is the Christian hope. And then will our bodies also rise from the dead. Yet not as fleshly bodies, but as spiritual bodies.

The expression which stands in the ancient Greek texts of the Apostles' Creed is quite certainly not biblical: "I believe in the resurrection of the flesh!"[27]

[26] Also to be understood in the light of this is F. J. Leenhardt's stu., "This is My Body," in Cullmann–Leenhardt, *Essays on the Lord's Supper* (Ecumenical Studies in Worship 1; 1958).

[27] W. Bieder, "Auferstehung des Leibes oder des Fleisches?," *Theol. Zeitschr.*, 1 (1945), pp. 105ff., seeks to explicate the expression "resurrection of the flesh," both from the point of view of biblical theology and of the history of dogma.

Paul could not say that. Flesh and blood cannot inherit the Kingdom. Paul believes in the resurrection of the *body*, not of the *flesh*. The flesh is the power of death, which must be destroyed. This error in the Greek creed made its entrance at a time when the biblical terminology had been misconstrued in the sense of Greek anthropology. Our body, moreover (not merely our soul), will be raised at the end, when the quickening power of the Spirit makes all things new, all things without exception.

An incorruptible body! How are we to conceive this? Or rather, how did the first Christians conceive of it? Paul says (Phil. 3:21) that at the end Christ will transform our lowly body into the body of his own glory (δόξα), just as in II Cor. 3:18: "We are being transformed into his own likeness from glory to glory (ἀπὸ δόξης εἰς δόξαν)." This glory (δόξα) was conceived by the first Christians as a sort of light-substance; but this is only an imperfect comparison. Our language has no word for it. Once again I refer to Grünewald's painting of the resurrection. He may have come closest to what Paul understood as the spiritual body.

IV. THOSE WHO SLEEP

The Holy Spirit and the Intermediate State of the dead

AND NOW WE come to the last question. When does this transformation of the body take place? No doubt can remain on this point. The whole New Testament answers, at the *end,* and this is to be understood literally, that is, in the temporal sense. That raises the question of the "interim condition" of the dead. Death is indeed already conquered according to II Tim. 1:10:

"Christ has conquered death and has already brought life and incorruptibility to light." The chronological tension, which I constantly stress, concerns precisely this central point: death is conquered, but it will not be abolished until the end. According to I Cor. 15:26, death will be conquered as the *last enemy*. It is significant that in the Greek the same verb καταργέω[28] is used to describe both the decisive victory already accomplished and the not-yet-consummated victory at the end. John's Apocalypse describes the victory at the end, the annihilation of death: "Death will be cast into a pool of fire" (Rev. 20:14); and a few verses farther on it is said, "Death will be no more."

That means, however, that the transformation of the body does not occur immediately after each individual death. Here too we must once again guard against any accommodation to Greek philosophy, if we wish to understand the New Testament doctrine. This is the point where I cannot accept Karl Barth's position as a simple restatement of the original Christian view, not even his position in the *Church Dogmatics*[29] where it is subtly shaded and comes much nearer[30] to New Testa-

[28] Luther translates καταργέω by "er hat ihm 'die Macht genommen'" in II Tim. 1:10, and by "er wird aufgehoben" in I Cor. 15:26.

[29] K. Barth, *Die kirchliche Dogmatik*, II, 1 (1940), pp. 698ff.; III, 2 (1948), pp. 524ff., 714ff.

[30] It is another question, of course, whether Barth does not have the *right* to adduce relationships in this whole matter which yet lie outside the New Testament circle of vision. But if so, then this "going beyond the New Testament" should perhaps be done consciously and should always be identified as such with clarity and emphasis, especially where a constant effort is being made to argue from the point of view of the Bible, as is the case with Barth. If this were done, then the inevitable danger which every dogmatician *must* confront (and here lies the dignity and greatness of his task) would be more clearly recognized: namely,

ment eschatology than in his first writings.[31] Karl
Barth considers it to be the New Testament interpretation that the transformation of the body occurs for
everyone immediately after his individual death—as if
the dead were no longer in time. Nevertheless, according to the New Testament, they *are* still in time.
Otherwise, the problem in I Thes. 4:13ff. would have
no meaning. Here in fact Paul is concerned to show
that at the moment of Christ's return "those who are
then alive will have no advantage" over those who have
died in Christ. Therefore the dead in Christ are still
in time; they, too, are *waiting*. "How long, Oh Lord?"
cry the martyrs who are sleeping under the altar (Rev.
6:10). Neither the saying on the cross, "Today you will
be with me in paradise" (Luke 23:43), the parable of
the rich man, where Lazarus is carried directly to Abraham's bosom (Luke 16:22), nor Paul's saying, "I desire
to die and to be with Christ" (Phil. 1:23), proves as
is often maintained that the resurrection of the body
takes place immediately after the individual death.[32]

---

the danger that he may not remain upon an extension of the
biblical line, but rather interpret the biblical texts primarily
ex post facto, from the point of view of his "going beyond the
New Testament." Precisely because of this clear recognition of
the danger, discussion with the exegete would be more fruitful.

[31] Especially *The Resurrection of the Dead* (1926).

[32] Also the much-disputed words of Luke 22:43, "Today you
will be with me in paradise," belong here. To be sure it is not
impossible, though artificial, to understand σήμερον (today) as
modifying λέγω σοι (I tell you). The statement is to be understood in the light of Luke 16:23 and of the Jewish conception of "paradise" as the place of the blessed (Strack-Billerbeck,
ad. loc.; P. Volz, *Die Eschatologie der jüdischen Gemeinde
im neutest. Zeitalter* [2nd ed., 1934], p. 265). It is certain
that Luke 16:23 does not refer to resurrection of the body,
and the expectation of the *Parousia* is in no way supplanted.
Such an interpretation is also decisively rejected by W. G.
Kümmel, *Promise and Fulfilment* (1957), p. 74. A certain

In none of these texts is there so much as a word about
the resurrection of the body. Instead, these different
images picture the condition of those who die in Christ
before the end—the interim state in which they, as well
as the living, find themselves. All these images express
simply a special proximity to Christ, in which those
dying in Christ before the end find themselves. They
are "with Christ" or "in paradise" or "in Abraham's
bosom" or, according to Rev. 6:9, "under the altar."
All these are simply various images of special nearness
to God. But the most usual image for Paul is: "They
are asleep."[33] It would be difficult to dispute that the
New Testament reckons with such an interim time for
the dead, as well as for the living, although any sort
of speculation upon the state of the dead in this
interim period is lacking here.

---

disparity here over against Pauline theology does exist insofar as Christ himself on the day referred to as "today" has not
yet risen, and therefore the foundation of the condition wherein
the dead are bound up with Christ has not yet been laid. But
in the last analysis the emphasis here is on the fact that the
thief will be *with Christ*. Menoud (*Le sort des trépassés*, p. 45)
correctly points out that Jesus' answer must be understood in
relation to the thief's entreaty. The thief asks Jesus to remember
him when he "comes into his kingdom," which according to the
Jewish view of the Messiah can only refer to the time when the
Messiah *will come* and erect his kingdom. Jesus does not grant
the request, but instead gives the thief more than he asked for:
he will be united *with Jesus* even before the coming of the
kingdom. So understood, *according to their intention*, these
words do not constitute a difficulty for the position maintained
above.

[33] The interpretation which K. Barth (*Die kirchliche Dogmatik*, III, 2, p. 778) gives of the "sleeping," as if this term
conveyed only the "impression" of a peaceful going to sleep
which those surviving have, finds no support in the New Testament. The expression in the New Testament signifies more, and
like the "repose" in Rev. 14:13 refers to the *condition* of the
dead before the Parousia.

The dead in Christ share in the tension of the interim time.[34] But this means not *only* that they are waiting. It means that for them, too, something decisive happened with Jesus' death and resurrection. For them, too, Easter is the great turning point (Matt. 27:52). This new situation created by Easter leads us to see at least the possibility of a common bond with Socrates, not with his teaching, but with his own behavior in the face of death. Death has lost its horror, its "sting." Though it remains as the last enemy, death has no longer any final significance. If the resurrection of Christ were to designate the great turning-point of the ages only for the living and not for the dead also, then the living would surely have an immense advantage over the dead. For as members of Christ's community the living are indeed even now in possession of the power of the resurrection, the Holy Spirit. It is unthinkable that, according to the early Christian point of view, nothing should be altered for the dead in the period before the end. It is precisely those images used in the New Testament to describe the condition of the dead in Christ which prove that even now, in this interim state of the dead, the resurrection of Christ— the anticipation of the end—is already effective. They are "with Christ."

Particularly in II Cor. 5:1–10 we hear why it is that the dead, although they do not yet have a body and are only "sleeping," nevertheless are in special prox-

---

[34] The lack of New Testament speculation on this does not give us the right simply to suppress the "interim condition" as such. I do not understand why Protestant theologians (including Barth) are so afraid of the New Testament position when the New Testament teaches only this much about the "interim condition": (1) that it exists, (2) that it already signifies union with Christ (this because of the Holy Spirit).

imity to Christ. Paul speaks here of the natural anxiety which even he feels before death, which still maintains its effectiveness. He fears the condition of "nakedness," as he calls it; that is, the condition of the inner man who has no body. This natural dread of death, therefore, has not disappeared. Paul would like, as he says, to receive a spiritual body in addition, directly (ἐπενδύσασθαι) while still living, without undergoing death. That is, he would like to be still alive at the time of Christ's return. Here once again we find confirmation of what we said about Jesus' fear of death. But now we see also something *new*: in this same text alongside this natural anxiety about the soul's nakedness stands the great confidence in Christ's proximity, *even in this interim state*. What is there to be afraid of in the fact that such an interim condition still exists? Confidence in Christ's proximity is grounded in the conviction that our inner man is already grasped by the Holy Spirit. Since the time of Christ, we, the living, do indeed have the Holy Spirit. If he is actually within us, he has already transformed our inner man. But, as we have heard, the Holy Spirit is the power of life. Death can do him no harm. Therefore something is indeed changed for the dead, for those who really die in Christ, i.e., in possession of the Holy Spirit. The horrible abandonment in death, the separation from God, of which we have spoken, no longer exists, precisely because the Holy Spirit does exist. Therefore the New Testament emphasizes that the dead are indeed *with Christ*, and so not abandoned. Thus we understand how it is that, just in II Cor. 5:1ff., where he mentions the fear of disembodiment in the interim time, Paul describes the Holy Spirit as the "earnest."

According to verse 8 of the same chapter, it even

appears that the dead are nearer Christ. The "sleep" seems to draw them even closer: "We are . . . willing rather to be absent from the body, and to be 'at home' with the Lord." For this reason, the apostle can write in Phil. 1:23 that he longs to die and be with Christ. So then, a man who lacks the fleshly body is yet nearer Christ than before, if he has the Holy Spirit. It is the flesh, bound to our earthly body, which is throughout our life the hindrance to the Holy Spirit's full development. Death delivers us from this hindrance even though it is an imperfect state inasmuch as it lacks the resurrection body. Neither in this passage nor elsewhere is found any more detailed information about this intermediate state in which the inner man, stripped indeed of its fleshly body but still deprived of the spiritual body, exists with the Holy Spirit. The apostle limits himself to assuring us that this state, anticipating the destiny which is ours once we have received the Holy Spirit, brings us closer to the final resurrection.

Here we find fear of a bodiless condition associated with firm confidence that even in this intermediate, transient condition no separation from Christ supervenes (among the powers which cannot separate us from the love of God in Christ is death—Rom. 8:38). This fear *and* this confidence are bound together in II Cor. 5, and this confirms the fact that even the dead share in the present tension. Confidence predominates, however, for the decision has indeed been made. Death is conquered. The inner man, divested of the body, is no longer alone; he does not lead the shadowy existence which the Jews expected and which cannot be described as life. The inner man, divested of the body, has already in his lifetime been transformed by the Holy Spirit, is already grasped by the resurrection

(Rom. 6:3ff., John 3:3ff.), if he *has* already as a living person really been renewed by the Holy Spirit. Although he still "sleeps" and still awaits the resurrection of the body, which alone will give him full life, the dead Christian *has* the Holy Spirit. Thus, even in this state, death has lost its terror, although it still exists. And so the dead who die in the Lord can actually be blessed "from now on" (ἀπ' ἄρτι),[35] as the author of the Johannine Apocalypse says (Rev. 14:13). What is said in I Cor. 15:54b, 55 pertains also to the dead: "Death is swallowed up in victory. O death, where is thy victory? O death, where is thy sting?" So Paul writes: "Whether we live or die, we belong to the Lord." Christ is "Lord of the living and the dead" (Rom. 14:8-9).

One could ask whether in this fashion we have not been led back again, in the last analysis, to the Greek doctrine of immortality, whether the New Testament does not assume, for the time after Easter, a continuity of the "inner man" of converted people before and after death, so that here, too, death is presented for all practical purposes only as a natural "transition."[36]

---

[35] In view of the places in the New Testament where ἀπ'ἄρτι can only mean "from now on" (for instance, John 13:19), and in view of the good sense which the sentence makes when ἀπ'ἄρτι is so translated, I continue to subscribe to the usual translation "from now on" and see it as modifying ἀποθνῄσκοντες, although many factors support A. Debrunner's view (Blass-Debrunner-Funk, *A Greek Grammar of the New Testament* [1961], §12), following A. Fridrichsen's suggestion, which understands ἀπαρτί as the colloquial Attic word for "exactly, certainly" and then finds in P47's omission of ναί a support for reading ἀπ'ἄρτι as ἀπαρτί, modifying λέγει τὸ πνεῦμα, not ἀποθνῄσκοντες.

[36] We have already spoken above of K. Barth's attempt (which indeed goes too far) to place a positive valuation in dialectical fashion alongside the negative valuation of death.

There is a sense in which a kind of *approximation* to the Greek teaching does actually take place, to the extent that the inner man, who has already been transformed by the Spirit (Rom. 6:3ff.), and consequently made alive, continues to live with Christ in this transformed state, in the condition of sleep. This continuity is emphasized especially strongly in the Gospel of John (3:36, 4:14, 6:54, and frequently). Here we observe at least a certain analogy to the "immortality of the soul," but the distinction remains none the less radical. Further, the condition of the dead in Christ is still imperfect, a state of "nakedness," as Paul says, of "sleep," of waiting for the resurrection of the whole creation, for the resurrection of the body. On the other hand, death in the New Testament continues to be the enemy, albeit a defeated enemy, who must yet be destroyed. The fact that even in this state the dead are already living with Christ does not correspond to the natural essence of the soul. Rather it is the result of a divine intervention from outside, through the Holy Spirit, who must already have quickened the inner man in earthly life by his miraculous power.

Thus it is still true that the resurrection of the body is awaited, even in John's Gospel—though now, of course, with a certainty of victory because the Holy Spirit already dwells in the inner man. Hence no doubt can arise any more: since he already dwells in the inner man, he will certainly transform the body. For the Holy Spirit, this quickening power, penetrates everything and knows no barrier. If he is really within a man, then he will quicken the whole man. So Paul writes in Rom. 8:11: "If the Spirit dwells in you, then will he who raised Christ Jesus from the dead call to life your mortal bodies also *through the Spirit dwelling*

in you." In Phil. 3:21: "We wait for the Lord Jesus
Christ, who will conform our lowly body to the body
of his glory." Nothing is said in the New Testament
about the details of the interim conditions. We hear
only this: we are nearer to God.

We wait, and *the dead* wait. Of course the rhythm
of time may be different for them than for the living;
and in this way the interim-time may be shortened for
them. This does not, indeed, go beyond the New Testament texts and their exegesis,[37] because this expression
to sleep, which is the customary designation in the
New Testament of the "interim condition," draws us
to the view that for the dead another time-conscious-
ness exists, that of "those who sleep." But that does
not mean that the dead are not still in time. Therefore
once again we see that the New Testament resurrection
hope is different from the Greek belief in immortality.

CONCLUSION

On his missionary journeys Paul surely met people who
were unable to believe in his preaching of the resurrection *for the very reason* that they believed in the immortality of the soul. Thus in Athens there was no
laughter until Paul spoke of the resurrection (Acts
17:32). Both the people of whom Paul says (in I Thes.
4:13) that "they have no hope" and those of whom he
writes (in I Cor. 15:12) that they do not believe there
is a resurrection from the dead are probably not Epicureans, as we are inclined to believe. Even those who
believe in the immortality of the soul do not have *the*
hope of which Paul speaks, the hope which expresses
the belief of a divine miracle of new creation which will

[37] Here I follow R. Mehl's suggestion, *Der letzte Feind*, p. 56.

embrace everything, every part of the world created by God. Indeed for the Greeks who believed in the immortality of the soul it may have been harder to accept the Christian preaching of the resurrection than it was for others. About the year 150 Justin writes of people "who say that there is no resurrection from the dead, but that immediately at death their souls would ascend to heaven" (Dialogue, 80). Here the contrast is indeed clearly perceived.

The emperor Marcus Aurelius, the philosopher who belongs with Socrates to the noblest figures of antiquity, also perceived the contrast. As is well known, he had the deepest contempt for Christianity. One might think that the death of the Christian martyrs would have inspired respect in this great Stoic who regarded death with equanimity. But it was just the martyrs' death with which he was least sympathetic. The alacrity with which the Christians met their death displeased him.[38] The Stoic departed this life dispassionately; the Christian martyr on the other hand died with spirited passion for the cause of Christ, because he knew that by doing so he stood within a powerful redemptive process. The first Christian martyr, Stephen, shows us (Acts 7:55) how very differently death is bested by him who dies in Christ than by the ancient philosopher: he sees, it is said, "the heavens open and Christ standing at the right hand of God!" He sees Christ, the conqueror of death. With this faith that the death he must undergo is already conquered by him who has himself endured it, Stephen lets himself be stoned.

The answer to the question, "Immortality of the

[38] M. Aurelius, *Med.*, XI, 3. To be sure, as time went on he more and more gave up the belief in the soul's immortality.

soul or resurrection of the dead in the New Testament," is unequivocal. The *teaching* of the great philosophers Socrates and Plato can in no way be brought into consonance with that of the New Testament. That their *person*, their *life*, and their *bearing in death* can nonetheless be *honored* by Christians, the apologists of the second century have shown. I believe it can also be demonstrated from the New Testament. But this is a question with which we do not have to deal here.

AFTERWORD[39]

A GERMAN edition of this Ingersoll Lecture was published in the *Festschrift* to Karl Barth,[40] and a summary has appeared in French periodicals. No other publication of mine has provoked such enthusiasm or such violent hostility. The editors of the periodicals concerned have been good enough to send me some of the letters of protest which they have received from their readers. One of the letter writers was prompted by my article to reflect bitterly that "the French people, dying for lack of the Bread of Life, have been offered instead of bread, stones, if not serpents." Another writer takes me for a kind of monster who delights in causing spiritual distress. "Has M. Cullmann," he writes, "a stone instead of a heart?" For a third, my

[39] EDITOR'S NOTE: When Professor Cullmann's Ingersoll Lecture was published in book form (London: The Epworth Press, 1958), it appeared with a 1956 preface, dated at Chamonix on September 15, in which the author took cognizance of the critique aroused by his views on the topic of resurrection and immortality. This preface is here reprinted as an Afterword.

[40] "Festgabe für Karl Barth zum 70. Geburtstag I," *Theol. Zeitschr.*, 12 (1956), pp. 126–56. See also *Verbum Caro* (1956), pp. 58ff.

study has been "the cause of astonishment, sorrow, and deep distress." Friends who have followed my previous work with interest and approval have indicated to me the pain which this study has caused them. In others I have detected a malaise which they have tried to conceal by an eloquent silence.

My critics belong to the most varied camps. The contrast, which out of concern for the truth I have found it necessary to draw between the courageous and joyful primitive Christian hope of the resurrection of the dead and the serene philosophic expectation of the survival of the immortal soul, has displeased not only many sincere Christians in all communions and of all theological outlooks, but also those whose convictions, while not outwardly alienated from Christianity, are more strongly molded by philosophical considerations. So far, no critic of either kind has attempted to refute me by exegesis, that being the basis of our study.

This remarkable agreement seems to me to show how widespread is the mistake of attributing to primitive Christianity the Greek belief in the immortality of the soul. Further, people with such different attitudes as those I have mentioned are united in a common inability to *listen* with complete objectivity to what the texts teach us about the faith and hope of primitive Christianity, without mixing their own opinions and the views that are so dear to them with their interpretation of the texts. This inability to listen is equally surprising on the part of intelligent people committed to the principles of sound, scientific exegesis and on the part of believers who profess to rely on the revelation in Holy Scripture.

The attacks provoked by my work would impress me more if they were based on exegetical arguments.

Instead, I am attacked with very general considerations of a philosophical, psychological, and, above all, sentimental kind. It has been said against me, "I can accept the immortality of the soul, but not the resurrection of the body," or "I cannot believe that our loved ones merely sleep for an indeterminate period, and that I myself, when I die, shall merely sleep while awaiting the resurrection."

Is it really necessary today to remind intelligent people, whether Christians or not, that there is a difference between recognizing that such a view was held by Socrates and accepting it, between recognizing a hope as primitive Christian and sharing it oneself?

We must first listen to what Plato and Paul said. We can go further. We can respect and indeed admire both views. How can we fail to do so when we see them in relation to the life and death of their authors? But that is no reason for denying a radical difference between the Christian expectation of the resurrection of the dead and the Greek belief in the immortality of the soul. However sincere our admiration for both views, it cannot allow us to pretend, against our profound conviction and against the exegetical evidence, that they arc compatible. That it is possible to discover certain points of contact, I have shown in this study; but that does not prevent their fundamental inspiration being totally different.

The fact that later Christianity effected a link between the two beliefs and that today the ordinary Christian simply confuses them has not persuaded me to be silent about what I, in common with most exegetes, regard as true; and all the more so, since the link established between the expectation of the "resurrection of the dead" and the belief in "the immortality of the soul" is not in fact a link at all but renunciation of one in favor of the other. I Cor. 15 has been sacrificed for the Phaedo. No good purpose is served by concealing this fact, as is often done today when things that are really incompatible are combined by the following type of oversimplified reasoning: that whatever in early Christian teaching appears to us irreconcilable with the immortality of the soul, viz., the resurrection of the body, is not an *essential* affirmation for the first Christians but simply an accommodation to the mythological expressions of the thought of their time, and that the heart of the matter is the immortality of the soul. On the contrary we must recognize loyally that precisely those things which distinguish the Christian teaching from the Greek belief are at the heart of primitive Christianity. Even if the interpreter cannot himself accept it as fundamental, he has no right to conclude that it was not fundamental for the authors whom he studies.

•   •   •   •

In view of the negative reactions and "distress" provoked by the publication of my thesis in various periodicals, should I not have broken off the debate for the sake of Christian charity, instead of publishing this booklet? My decision has been determined by the conviction that "stumbling blocks" are sometimes salutary, both from the scholarly and the Christian point of view. I simply ask my readers to be good enough to take the trouble of reading on till the end.

The question is here raised in its exegetical aspect. If we turn to the Christian aspect, I would venture to remind my critics that when they put in the forefront, as they do, the particular manner in which they *wish* themselves and their loved ones to survive, they are involuntarily giving grounds to the opponents of Christianity who constantly repeat that the faith of Christians is nothing more than the projection of their desires.

In reality, does it not belong to the greatness of our Christian faith, as I have done my best to expound it, that we do not begin from our personal desires but place our resurrection within the framework of a cosmic redemption and of a new creation of the universe?

I do not underestimate in any way the difficulty one may experience in sharing this faith, and I freely admit the difficulty of talking about this subject in a dispassionate manner. An open grave at once reminds us that we are not simply concerned with a matter of academic discussion. But is there not therefore all the more reason for seeking truth and clarity at this point? The best way to do it is not by beginning with what is ambiguous, but by explaining simply and as faithfully as possible, with all the means at our disposal, the hope of the New Testament authors, and thus showing the very essence of this hope and—however hard it may seem to us—what it is that separates it from other beliefs we hold so dear. If in the first place we examine objectively the primitive Christian expectation in those aspects which seem shocking to our commonly accepted views, are we not following the only possible way by which it may perhaps nonetheless be given us, not only to understand that expectation better, but also to ascertain that it is not so impossible to accept it as we imagine.

I have the impression that some of my readers have not troubled to read my exposition right through. The comparison of the death of Socrates with that of Jesus seems to have scandalized and irritated them so much that they have read no farther, and have not looked at what I have said about the New Testament faith in the victory of Christ over death.

For many of those who have attacked me, the cause of "sorrow and distress" has been not only the distinction we draw between resurrection of the dead and immortality of the soul, but above all the place which I with the whole of primitive Christianity believe should be given to the intermediate state of those who are dead and die in Christ before the final days, the state which the first-century authors described by the word "sleep." The idea of a temporary state of waiting is all the more repugnant to those who would like fuller information about this "sleep" of the dead who, though stripped of their fleshly bodies, are still deprived of their resurrection bodies although in possession of the Holy Spirit. They are not able to observe the discretion of the New Testament authors, including Paul, in this matter; or to be satisfied with the joyful assurance of the Apostle when he says that henceforth death can no longer separate from Christ him who has the Holy Spirit. "Whether we live or die, we belong to Christ."

There are some who find this idea of "sleep" entirely unacceptable. I am tempted to lay aside for a moment the exegetical methods of this study and ask them whether they have never experienced a dream which has made them happier than any other experience, even though they have only been sleeping. Might that not be an illustration, though indeed an imperfect one, of the state of anticipation in which, according to Paul, the dead in Christ find themselves during their "sleeping" as they wait for the resurrection of the body?

However that may be, I do not intend to avoid the "stumbling block" by minimizing what I have said about the provisional and still imperfect character of this state. The fact is that, according to the first Christians the full, genuine life of the resurrection is inconceivable apart from the new body, the "spiritual body," with which the dead will be clothed when heaven and earth are re-created.

In this study I have referred more than once to the Isenheim altarpiece by the medieval painter Grünewald. It was the resurrection body that he depicted, not the immortal soul. Similarly, another artist, Johann Sebastian Bach, has made it possible for us to hear, in the Credo of the Mass in B Minor, the musical interpretation of the words of this ancient creed which faithfully reproduces the New Testament faith in Christ's resurrection and our own. The jubilant music of this great composer is intended to express not the immortality of the soul but the event of the resurrection of the body: *Et resurrexit tertia die. . . . Expecto resurrectionem mortuorum et vitam venturi saeculi.* And Handel, in the last part of the *Messiah*, gives us some inkling of what Paul understood by the sleep of those who rest in Christ; and also, in the song of triumph, Paul's expectation of the final resurrection when the "last trumpet shall sound and we shall be changed."

Whether we share this hope or not, let us at least admit that in this case the artists have proved the best expositors of the Bible.

IMMORTALITY AND RESURRECTION IN THE PHILOSOPHY OF THE CHURCH FATHERS

THE INGERSOLL LECTURE FOR 1956

Harry A. Wolfson

LAST year, on this platform, under the auspices of this lectureship, an eminent New Testament scholar, Professor Oscar Cullmann, depicted for us two scenes. One scene was laid in Athens, in a prison, where Socrates awaited death cheerfully, courageously, and without complaint. This cheerful, courageous, and uncomplaining attitude of Socrates toward death, said Professor Cullmann, was due to his belief in the immortality of the soul. The other scene was laid in Jerusalem, at Gethsemane and Golgotha, where Jesus awaited death amazedly,[1] sorrowfully,[2] and "with strong crying and tears."[3] From this, Professor Cullmann inferred that Jesus did not believe in the immortality of the soul; that to him death meant the death of both body and soul; and hence that resurrection, in which he explicitly expresses a belief, meant to him a new creation of soul as well as of body.[4]

Let us depict for you another scene, one laid not in

[1] Mark 14:33.
[2] Matt. 26:37, 38.
[3] Heb. 5:7.
[4] Cf. Professor Cullmann's essay in this volume, pp. 9–53.

54

far-off Athens about 492 years before the Crucifixion but in a village about thirty miles from the place of the Crucifixion and only about half a century after its occurrence.

We are told[5] that when Rabban Johanan, the son of Zakkai, fell ill and was about to die, his disciples came to visit him. Upon seeing them, he began to weep. His disciples said to him: "Light of Israel, right pillar, mighty hammer, wherefore weepest thou?" In his answer he explained that he wept because his soul, which would survive his body, would have to face the inscrutable judgment of the supreme King of Kings, the Holy One, blessed be He.

This, ladies and gentlemen, is exactly the reason why Jesus awaited death amazedly, sorrowfully, and "with strong crying and tears." It is because he believed his soul was immortal and would have to face the inscrutable judgment of the Lord his God, the Most High; for, even though, as we are told, "in him is no sin,"[6] certainly there was not in him the sin of being righteous in his own eyes.

But whatever one may be pleased to prove with regard to what Jesus thought of immortality and resurrection, to thc Fathers of the Church these two beliefs were inseparably connected with each other. To them, the belief that Jesus rose on the third day after the Crucifixion meant that his soul survived the death of the body and was reinvested with his risen body. Similarly the belief that in the end of days there will be a general resurrection of the dead meant the reinvestment of surviving souls with risen bodies. To all of them, in the interval between death and resurrection,

[5] *Berakot* 28b.
[6] I John 3:5.

the soul had a life of its own without a body, though there was some difference of opinion as to what was the state of the soul's life during that interval. And this conception of resurrection as implying immortality was attributed by the Fathers also to Jesus. Accordingly the verse, "I am the God of Abraham and the God of Isaac and the God of Jacob,"[7] which Jesus, in his answer to the challenge of the Sadducees, used as a proof-text for the belief in resurrection,[8] was used by Church Fathers like Justin Martyr[9] and Irenaeus[10] as proof-text for both resurrection and immortality. And in their effort to strengthen the belief in immortality and the belief in resurrection as Christian doctrines, the Fathers not only followed the example of their Master in trying to prove, by quoting additional verses, that these beliefs have their roots in the Old Testament, but they also went beyond the Master's example and undertook to show that these beliefs were not contrary to reason. With this in view, they set out in search of philosophic testimonials for immortality and resurrection.[11]

With regard to immortality, the Fathers did not have to go far afield in their search. This belief is writ large upon the pages of Plato's *Phaedo* and it peers out from between the lines of other philosophic writings. But already forewarned by Philo, or reasoning like Philo from the same scriptural principles, the Fathers knew

[7] Exod. 3:6.
[8] Matt. 22:23–32; Mark 12:27; Luke 20:37.
[9] *Apologia* I, 63.
[10] *Adv. Haer.* IV, 5, 2.
[11] Certain parts of the discussion which follows deal with topics which I have treated more fully in the as yet unpublished Volume II of *The Philosophy of the Church Fathers*.

that the Platonic philosophic conception of immortality is not exactly the same as the scriptural conception of it. To Plato, immortality belonged to the soul by nature, for by its very nature the soul could not be mortal. In Scripture, immortality was a gift or grace of God to the soul, for by its own nature the soul was mortal.[12] This distinction between the Platonic and the scriptural conception of immortality is constantly stressed by the Fathers. One of the first of the Fathers to discuss this problem, Justin Martyr, commenting upon the statement that "according to some who are termed Platonists," the soul is immortal,[13] says, "I pay no regard to Plato," and then, proceeding to expound what he considers "the truth" of the matter, argues, evidently against Plato's conception of immortality, that, if the soul lives, "it lives not as being itself life, but as the partaking of life," and this because "God wills it to live, and hence it will cease to live whenever he may please that it shall live no longer, for it is not the property of the soul to have life in itself as it is the property of God."[14] The same view is expressed also by Irenaeus,[15] Tatian,[16] Theophilus,[17] Arnobius,[18] Lactantius,[19] and others.

Occasionally, indeed, some of the Fathers use language loosely, so that what they say, when taken out of its context, may lead to a misunderstanding of their

---

[12] Cf. my *Philo*, 3rd ed., rev. (Cambridge, Mass., 1962).
[13] *Dial. cum Tryph.* 5.
[14] *Ibid.* 6.
[15] *Adv. Haer.* II 34, 4.
[16] *Orat. ad Graec.* 13.
[17] *Ad Autol.* II, 27; cf. II, 24.
[18] *Adv. Gent.* II, 14, 32.
[19] *Div. Inst.* VII, 5.

view. Thus three Fathers, at least, have been misunderstood and taken to believe that the soul is immortal by its own nature.[20] The first of these Fathers who gave rise to a misunderstanding is Tertullian, and this because he speaks of the soul as being "immortal by nature" (*immortalis natura*)[21] and of immortality as being one of the things that are "known by nature" (*natura nota*).[22] But the context of the passages in which these expressions occur makes it clear that by the first expression Tertullian means that the soul "cannot be killed by men"[23] and by the second expression he means that the belief in the immortality of the soul can be attained by natural reason "from common notions" (*de communibus sensibus*).[24] When, therefore, in explanation of his use of his second expression, he says, "I may use, therefore, the opinion of Plato, when he declares, 'Every soul is immortal,'"[25] he does not mean that he agrees with the Platonic conception of the immortality of the soul; it only means that Plato has arrived at his conception of immortality, imperfect though it be, by natural reason. In still another place, Tertullian explains that the expression "that which was lost" (*quod periit*, τὸ ἀπολωλός) in the verse that the "Son of man is come to seek and to save that which was lost,"[26] if referred to the

[20] Cf. A. Stöckl, *Geschichte der Philosophie der patristischen Zeit* (1859), pp. 197, 235, 393; *Geschichte der christlichen Philosophie zur Zeit der Kirchenväter* (1891), pp. 136f., 168f., 338f.; W. Capitaine, *Die Moral des Clemens von Alexandria* (1903), pp. 119f.

[21] *De Resur. Carn.* 35.

[22] *Ibid.* 3.

[23] *Ibid.* 35.

[24] *Ibid.* 3.

[25] *Ibid.*

[26] Luke 19:10.

soul, means not "destruction" but "punishment," and this on the ground that the soul "is safe already in its own nature by reason of its immortality."[27] Here, it is only the "safety" of the soul and not its "immortality" that is described by him as being "in its own nature"; the immortality itself is conceived by him, as by all other Fathers, as being a gift of God, a gift which, while God could take away, he will not take away. This, as we shall see, is the view also of some other Fathers, and among those they who explicitly deny that the soul is immortal by nature.[28] Nor, finally, does his statement that the soul is indivisible because it is immortal[29] mean that its immortality, which is the cause of its indivisibility, is itself by nature and not by the will of God. It only means that inasmuch as the soul is endowed by God with immortality, by virtue of its immortality it is also indivisible.

Origen is another who is alleged to have believed that the soul is immortal by its own nature, and this because of his speaking of "the essence" (*substantia*) of the human soul as being immortal and of his explaining its immortality as being due to the fact that it "partakes" of the divine nature[30] and because also of his repudiating anyone who ventures to ascribe to it "essential (*substantialis*) corruption."[31] But all this only means, as may be gathered from his reply to Celsus,[32] that the soul, having been created by God as partaking of his own nature, will not be destroyed by

[27] *De Resur. Carn.* 34.
[28] Cf., for instance, Lactantius in the passages referred to above n. 19 and below n. 54.
[29] *De Anima* 14 and 51.
[30] *De Princip.* IV, 9 (36).
[31] *Ibid.* IV, 10 (37).
[32] Cf. *Cont. Cels.* V, 22, and below at n. 168.

God; it does not mean that God could not destroy it, if he so willed.

The third Father who is supposed to have believed that the soul is immortal by nature is Augustine, and this evidently because, in his *De Immortalitate Animae* and *Soliloquia*, he attempts to prove the immortality of the soul by arguments which are reminiscent of those used by Plato and Plotinus in proving that the soul is immortal by nature. But the use of philosophic arguments by any Father in support of a religious doctrine does not necessarily mean that his conception of that religious doctrine is the same as the conclusion which philosophers sought to establish by those arguments. What Augustine's own conception of immortality was may be gathered from his statement that though "the soul of man is, according to a peculiar sense of its own (*secundum quemdam modum suum*), immortal, it is not absolutely immortal as God is, of whom it is written that he 'alone hath immortality' "[33] and as he proceeds he explains that the soul is described as being, "according to a peculiar sense of its own, immortal" and as "not wholly ceasing to live by its own nature"[34] only in the sense that it is not annihilated, that is to say, it is not annihilated by God, who by his will had brought it into existence and who could, therefore, annihilate it, if he so willed.

While the Fathers found direct philosophic support for immortality, no such support could they find for resurrection. Pseudo-Justin Martyr declares that "the Greeks refuse to believe" in resurrection and, when he

[33] I Tim. 6:16.
[34] *Epistolae* 166, 2, 3. Cf. *De Natura Boni* 39; *De Genesi ad Litteram* VII, 28, 43.

thought that in the myth of the punishment of Aridaeus, as retold by Plato, he had discovered traces of a belief in resurrection, he said, "Here Plato seems to me to have learned from the prophets not only the doctrine of the judgment but also that of resurrection."[35] Cyril of Jerusalem, speaking of resurrection, proclaims that "Greeks contradict it,"[36] and Augustine complains that, while "on the immortality of the soul many gentile philosophers have disputed at great length and in many books they have left it written that the soul is immortal, when they came to the resurrection of the flesh, they doubt not indeed, but they most openly deny it, describing it to be absolutely impossible that this earthly flesh can ascend to heaven."[37] Still, while they could find no direct support for resurrection, they found in the teachings of philosophers two doctrines which were cited by some of the Fathers as two analogies of the Christian doctrine of resurrection.

The first analogy is the Stoic doctrine of palingenesis or regeneration, according to which in the infinite succession of destroyed and created worlds each newly arising world is an exact duplicate of the past destroyed world, so that every individual who died in one world will be regenerated exactly in the same way in every other world. Socrates and Xanthippe, Plato and his successor, Speusippus, Aristotle and Alexander, all of whom were born and lived and died in this world of ours, had already repeatedly been born and lived and died in the infinite succession of worlds before this world of ours and will repeatedly be born and live and

---

[35] *Cohortatio ad Graecos* 27; c. Plato, *Republic* X, 615C-616A.

[36] *Catecheses* XVIII, 1.

[37] *Enarr. in Psalm.* 88, 5 (PL 37, 1134).

die in the infinite successive worlds after this of ours. An analogy between these two beliefs is sometimes suggested by the Fathers themselves. Thus Tatian[38] and Clement of Alexandria[39] and Origen[40] hint at such an analogy, and Lactantius[41] and Augustine[42] explicitly advance it as proof for the possibility of resurrection, and Nemesius quotes it as something said by "some people."[43] But having hinted at or mentioned this analogy, the Fathers who happened to discuss it further tried to show that these two beliefs are not exactly the same. The essential difference between these two beliefs, mentioned explicitly in Tatian, Augustine, and Nemesius and implied in Origen and Lactantius, is that the Stoic palingenesis means an infinite succession of resurrections to a temporary life, whereas the Christian resurrection means one resurrection to an eternal life. The philosophic basis of this essential difference, as stated by Tatian, is that the Stoic palingenesis is an endless repetition of the same thing "for no useful purpose," whereas the Christian resurrection is "for the purpose of passing judgment." The same view is also more or less clearly expressed by Augustine, Nemesius, Origen, and Lactantius. In other words, to the Stoics, it is an act of fate or necessity or what they would also call an act of nature; to the Christians, it is an act of divine will and design.

The second philosophic analogy is the theory of the transmigration of souls, which the Fathers usually

[38] Orat. ad Graec. 6.
[39] Stromata V, 1. 9 (PG 9, 21A). Section reference here and in the notes below is to ed. Stählin.
[40] Cont. Cels. V, 20.
[41] Div. Inst. VII, 23.
[42] De Civ. Dei XXII, 28.
[43] De Natura Hominis 38 (PG 40, 761A).

attribute to such philosophers as Pythagoras, Empedocles, and Plato. Tertullian describes it as a belief which "most nearly approaches" the Christian doctrine of resurrection.[44] Origen quotes Celsus as having taunted the Christians that their doctrine of resurrection has its origin in a misunderstanding of "the doctrine of the transmigration of souls."[45] Gregory of Nyssa says that the philosophic theory of transmigration of souls is "not absolutely out of harmony with the resurrection which we hope for."[46] Similar assumptions as to the analogy between these two beliefs are to be found also in Irenaeus,[47] Lactantius,[48] and Augustine.[49] Here, again, having become conscious of the analogy between these two beliefs, the Fathers undertake to show that the two beliefs are not exactly the same. The difference found by them between these two beliefs is that in transmigration, the soul enters another human body or even the body of an animal or a plant, whereas resurrection means the return of souls to their own restored bodies.[50]

From these discussions by the Fathers, as well as from their discussions in other places of their writings, we may gather that, according to them, two principles are to be regarded as distinctive characteristics of the Christian conception of immortality and resurrection. First, both immortality and resurrection are volitional

---

[44] De Resur. Carn. 1.
[45] Cont. Cels. VII, 32.
[46] De An. et Resur. (PG 46, 108D).
[47] Adv. Haer. II, 33, 1; Cf. II, 34, 1.
[48] Div. Inst. VII, 23.
[49] De Civ. Dei XXII, 27.
[50] Cf. Irenaeus, loc. cit.; Tertullian, Apologeticus 48; Origen, loc. cit.; Lactantius, loc. cit.; Augustine, loc. cit.

acts of God and not necessary acts of nature. Second, in resurrection the body risen to life must be identical with the body that had existed before.

Each of these principles gave rise to a question, and each question gave rise to various answers.

The first principle, that of volition, implying as it does that if God willed, He could bring annihilation to the soul as well as withhold resurrection from the body, gave rise to the question whether God will ever will to annihilate a soul. Now to ascertain the will of God on any of such matters one must go first to consult the oracles of Scripture. But the oracle of Delphi on any question are as vague as the oracle of Delphi on any question and, if not vague, then they are downright contradictory. According to one set of scriptural utterances, the wicked will suffer "everlasting punishment" (κόλασις αἰώνιος);[51] according to another set of utterances they are destined to everlasting "destruction" (ὄλεθρος)[52] or "perdition" (ἀπώλεια).[53] And so the Fathers had their choice, either to follow the verses which threaten the wicked with "destruction" and make those which threaten them with "punishment" yield to some kind of interpretation, or the other way around. No unanimity of opinion was arrived at by the Fathers. The generality of them felt that eternal punishment is that which the wicked deserve and tried to show that the "destruction" and "perdition" could not have meant annihilation.[54] Arnobius, on the other hand, felt that the punishment which the wicked

---

[51] Matt. 25:46; John 5:29; Rom. 2:8, 9.
[52] II Thes. 1:9; cf. I Thes. 5:3.
[53] Rom. 9:22; Phil. 3:19; II Thes. 2:3; Heb. 10:39; II Pet. 3:7; cf. Matt. 7:13.
[54] Cf. Tertullian, De Resur. Carn. 35; Lactantius, Div. Inst. VII, 11; Augustine, Epist. 166, 2, 3.

deserve is annihilation.[55] Origen, however, is opposed
not only to annihilation[56] but also to a punishment
which is eternal, contending that there will be a final
restoration of all the wicked who are dead,[57] and, as
for the term "everlasting" (αἰώνιος), by which the term
"punishment" is described in the New Testament, he
tried to show that that Greek term in the New Testament, like its corresponding Hebrew term 'olam in the
Old Testament, is to be taken to mean not everlasting
but a very long time.[58]

The other principle, that of identity, gave rise to the
question of how to reconcile it with certain verses in
the New Testament which would seem to teach that
the resurrected bodies would not be identical with
their respective counterparts before death. The verses
which are usually brought into play in this connection
are two: (1) Jesus' statement concerning those who
will rise that "in the resurrection they . . . are as the
angels of God in heaven"[59] or "equal unto angels";[60]
(2) Paul's statement concerning the body as buried
and the body as risen that "it is sown a natural
(ψυχικόν) body; it is raised a spiritual (πνευματικόν)
body."[61] Of the various views found among the Fathers
on the principle of identity, we shall deal here only
with two.

The first view is that of Origen. As his starting point,
he takes the words of Jesus and Paul we have just
quoted. Drawing upon Paul's description of that body

[55] Adv. Gent. II, 14.
[56] De Princip. IV, 4, 9 (36).
[57] Ibid. I, 6.
[58] In Exod., Hom. 6, 13.
[59] Matt. 22:30; Mark 12:25.
[60] Luke 20:36.
[61] I Cor. 15:44.

as "spiritual" and upon Jesus' description of it as being "as the angels of God" or "equal unto angels," he says that the "sons of resurrection," even as the "angels of God," will be adorned "with the clothing of a spiritual body,"[62] and as such it will differ from the "animal body" of man during his first lifetime on earth.[63] Wishing, however, to preserve the principle of identity, he says that the resurrected body, with all its being spiritual, is not a new and different body. It is still essentially the same as the original animal body. We are to believe, Origen maintains, that the body "which we now make use of in a state of meanness and corruption and weakness, is not a different body from that which we shall possess in incorruption and in power and in glory,"[64] for "we are to hold that this very body which now, on account of its service to the soul, is styled an animal body, will—by means of a certain progress, when the soul has been united to God and made one spirit with him so that the body is then rendering service as it were to the spirit—attain a spiritual condition and quality."[65]

But what is that which remains undestroyed throughout the change of the body from its being animal to its being spiritual, so as to serve as a common element in the two successive states of the body and thus to constitute its identity? Origen gives two answers to this question, which two answers, however, may be considered as complementing one another and as constituting two steps in one single argument.

The first step in the argument is to establish that

62 *De Princip.* II, 2, 2; cf. I, 8, 4.
63 *Ibid.* II, 10, 1; II, 10, 3.
64 *Ibid.* III, 6, 6.
65 *Ibid.*

there is an element which is common to sublunar bodies, celestial bodies, and the so-called spiritual bodies, such as angels and resurrected bodies. Whatever differences there are between them are not differences in kind but only differences in degree, described by him as differences in the degree of purity (*puritas*) or of subtileness (*subtilitas*) or of glory (*gloria*).[66] This common element is called by him "ether"—a term which is used by Plato in the sense of one of the four elements, air,[67] and by Aristotle in the sense of a fifth element.[68] Origen, preferring to follow Plato, uses it in the sense of one of the four elements, air,[69] and, referring to the Aristotelian conception of ether as a fifth element constituting the celestial bodies, he says that "the faith of the Church" is against "certain Grecian philosophers" who believe that "there is besides the body composed of four elements another fifth element, which is different in all its parts and diverse from this one present body."[70] Accordingly, the celestial bodies, angels, and the resurrected bodies are all described by him as ethereal, with the understanding, of course, that they are of different grades of purity or subtileness or glory. Even among the various celestial bodies, he remarks, do such differences exist.[71] There is thus an element which is common to our present animal body and our future spiritual body.

But this element, Origen must have felt, is common to all bodies and consequently, while the assumption of the existence of such an element establishes negatively

[66] *Ibid.* III, 6, 4.
[67] *Timaeus* 58D; *Phaedo* 111A.
[68] *De Caelo* I, 3, 270b, 22.
[69] *De Princip.* II, 1, 1.
[70] *Ibid.* III, 6, 6.
[71] *Ibid.* II, 10, 2.

the fact that resurrected spiritual bodies are not generically different from animal bodies before their death, it does not establish an identity between any individual resurrected spiritual body and its corresponding animal body before its death. In the second step of his argument, Origen, therefore, undertakes to analyze the concept of identity with a view to showing that such an identity exists between the animal and the spiritual body.

When identity is asserted of any given body, he seems to argue, it does not mean that that body remains the same in every respect. No human being, even during man's lifetime, retains a body which remains the same in every detail: it undergoes changes in size, in color, in weight, and in many other similar respects. What is it then that constitutes the identity of any individual body? Plunging himself into the problem of the principle of individuation, on which there is to be found in Aristotle a variety of statements, Origen maintains, not in opposition to Aristotle, I think, but rather as an interpretation of him, that the principle of individuation is not the underlying proximate matter ($\pi\rho\hat{\omega}\tau\text{o}\nu$ $\hat{\upsilon}\pi\text{o}\kappa\epsilon\acute{\iota}\mu\epsilon\nu\text{o}\nu$) but rather the form ($\tau\grave{\text{o}}$ $\epsilon\hat{\iota}\delta\text{o}\varsigma$). But that form is taken by him not as something common to all members of the species, as the Greek term for form, $\epsilon\hat{\iota}\delta\text{o}\varsigma$, would imply, but as something peculiar to a single member of a species as its individual property, a sort of individual form added to a specific form. Origen thus describes that form as "the characteristic form" ($\tau\grave{\text{o}}$ $\epsilon\hat{\iota}\delta\text{o}\varsigma$ $\tau\grave{\text{o}}$ $\chi\alpha\rho\alpha\kappa\tau\eta\rho\acute{\iota}\zeta\text{o}\nu$), that is to say, the form which stamps individual bodies with distinctive characteristics, inhering in them as one of their peculiar properties ($\hat{\iota}\delta\iota\acute{\omega}\mu\alpha\tau\alpha$) and molding them into permanent impressions ($\tau\acute{\upsilon}\pi\text{o}\iota$), that is to say, into

permanent individualized impressions. It is this individual form of the animal body that is reunited with the
soul at the time of the resurrection.[72] This individual
form is described by Origen as a "reason" (*ratio*)
which, like "the power (*virtus*) which is in the grain
of wheat," is implanted in our bodies and contains a
"bodily substance" (*substantia corporalis*) out of which
a body will arise on the day of resurrection.[73] This
individual form or "reason" (*ratio*) is also described by
him more fully by the Stoic expression "seminal reason"
(λόγος σπέρματος = σπερματικός).[74] Thus the resurrected
spiritual body has, according to him, the same individuality as the animal body of its former existence. But
the sameness of individuality does not mean that it has
the same figure and shape and limbs and organs and
those other appurtenances of the animal body.[75]

The extreme opposite of this is the view of the generality of the Fathers. All of them stress identity in its
literal sense as the main principle in the Christian conception of the resurrected body. While Tatian merely
says that God, "when He pleases, will restore the substance that is visible to him alone to its pristine
condition,"[76] Irenaeus expresses himself more clearly
in his description of those rising at the general resurrection that they will rise "with their very own
bodies."[77] Still more explicit is Tertullian when he
maintains that "the flesh shall rise again, wholly, in
every man, in its identity, in its absolute integrity,"[78]

[72] *In Psalm.* I, 5 (PG 12, 1093B–C).
[73] *De Princip.* II, 10, 3.
[74] *Cont. Cels.* VII, 32 (PG 11, 1465A).
[75] *Ibid.* V, 19; VII, 32; *In Psalm.* I, 5.
[76] *Orat. ad Graec.* 6.
[77] *Adv. Haer.* II, 33, 5; cf. II, 34, 1.
[78] *De Resur. Carn.* 63.

retaining all the parts of our body, the various limbs, such as mouth, teeth, throat, stomach, belly, bowels, hands, feet, and also the differences of sex, with the various organs of generation in the two sexes.[79] Cyril of Jerusalem insists that the body that will be raised will be the very same body (αὐτὸ τοῦτο).[80] Gregory of Nyssa, speaking through St. Macrina, defines resurrection as "the restitution of our nature to its original form,"[81] which means, as may be gathered from its context, that the body will arise fully equipped with all its organs. Augustine similarly insists that those who will rise "will be bodies and not spirits" and that "as far as regards substance, even then it shall be flesh,"[82] maintaining, furthermore, like Tertullian, that there will be a distinction of sex among those who will rise.[83]

But, if the resurrected body will be exactly the same as it was before death, what then is the meaning of Jesus' statement that those who will rise will be "as the angels of God" or "equal unto angels" and of Paul's statement that they will have a "spiritual body"?

The question is discussed by many Fathers.

As for the description of the resurrected body as angels, Tertullian points out that Jesus did not say that they shall be "angels"; he only said "equal unto angels,"[84] which, he argues, merely means that, while possessing the same body as that before they died, they shall "no more be exposed to the usual solicitations of the flesh in their angelic garb," especially mentioning the fact that, like angels, they shall be "not marrying,

---

[79] Ibid. 60.
[80] Catecheses XVIII. 18.
[81] De An. et Resur. (PG 46, 148A, 155C).
[82] Enchiridion 91.
[83] De Civ. Dei XXII, 17.
[84] De Resur. Carn. 62.

because of not dying."[85] Augustine toward the end of
his life declared that his earlier statement that "we
ought to believe that the angelic bodies which we hope
to inhabit are most luminous and ethereal"[86] should
not be taken to mean that "we shall not have the same
members of the body or the same substance of our
flesh."[87] And as for the use of the term "spiritual,"
Augustine explains that it is not because the resurrected
body "is converted into spirit, as some fancy," but
"because it is subject to the spirit with a perfect and
marvelous readiness of obedience," for, "as when the
spirit serves the flesh, it is fitly called carnal, so, when
the flesh serves the spirit, it will justly be called
spiritual."[88] Gregory of Nyssa, with reference to the
description of the resurrected as both angelic and
spiritual explains that "all that blessed state which
arises for us by means of the resurrection is only a
return to our pristine state of grace,"[89] that is, to the
state of Adam before his fall.

This conception of a body fully equipped with all
its members but resurrected to a life in which none of
these members will be needed for the preservation of
that life, gave rise to a question which is expressed by
Tertullian as follows: "What will be the use of the
entire body, when the entire body shall become useless?"[90] Back of this question is Plato's explanation[91]
of how every bodily organ has a certain utility for the
preservation and perpetuation of life as well as

[85] *Ibid.*
[86] *De Diversis Quaestionibus* LXXXVIII, 47.
[87] *Retractiones* I, 26.
[88] *De Civ. Dei* XIII, 20.
[89] *De An. et Resur.* (PG 46, 156D).
[90] *De Resur. Carn.* 60.
[91] Cf. *Timaeus* 70–76.

Aristotle's statement that "God and nature do nothing in vain."[92] After trying at various answers, Tertullian finally concludes with this general statement: "If, indeed, it has existence, it will be quite possible for it not to be useless; it may possibly have something to do; for in the presence of God there will be no idleness."[93] In other words, it must be assumed that the organs in the resurrected body will serve some purpose, though what that purpose will be is known only to God and it is past our understanding. Similarly Gregory of Nyssa, after describing, in the manner not only of Plato but also of Galen,[94] how the various members of the body have their special useful operations, raises, with regard to the resurrected, the following question: "When, therefore, all these operations will be no more, how and wherefore will their instruments exist?"[95] His answer is like that of Tertullian. "The true explanation of all these questions," he says, "is still stored up in the hidden treasure-rooms of Wisdom, and will not come to light until that moment when we shall be taught the mystery of the resurrection by the reality of it; and then there will be no more need of phrases to explain the things which we now hope for."[96]

This then is what the Fathers believed about immortality and resurrection and this is how, whenever necessary, they explained themselves philosophically.

But the Fathers, learned in philosophy as many of them were, knew that besides those philosophers who believed in immortality, there were others, chief among

[92] De Caelo I, 4, 271a, 33.
[93] De Resur. Carn. 60.
[94] Cf. De Usu Partium Corporis Humani.
[95] De An. et Resur. (PG 46, 144D-145A).
[96] Ibid. (PG 46, 145B).

them the Epicureans, who were outspoken opponents of immortality and argued against it. While no formal and direct refutation of the Epicurean arguments is to be found, as far as I could ascertain, in the Fathers of the Church, answers in anticipation of those arguments are provided by them in their discussions of the nature, origin, and functions of the soul as well as in their positive arguments for immortality. Let us then see how the Fathers would answer the Epicurean arguments against immortality.

One of the Epicurean arguments against immortality is that the soul is corporeal, composed as it is, according to the Epicurean view, of atoms, and that it is born, grows, and ages with the body, and therefore it is dissolved with the body.[97]

An indirect answer to this argument, or an answer in anticipation of this argument, may be found in the Fathers' discussion of the nature and the origin of the soul.

Superficially, on the basis of the language in which the Fathers express themselves, it would seem that they are divided into two camps on the question of the nature of the soul. In one camp are the majority of the Fathers who argue that the soul is incorporeal. In the other camp is Tertullian, who, in splendid isolation, or perhaps with a few insignificant camp followers, maintains that the soul is corporeal, and, quoting the Stoics, he rejects altogether the use of the term incorporeal. The contrast between these two camps emerges all the bolder when both these camps are found to bolster up their respective views by the same scriptural proof-text. The proof-text is the verse, "And the Lord God . . . breathed into his nostrils the breath (*nishmat,* πνοήν,

[97] Lucretius, *De Rerum Natura* III, 418–458.

spiraculum) of life."[98] The question arose: What does the term "breath" or *neshamah* or πνοή or *spiraculum* mean? Most Fathers, following Philo, say it means something which is not body, something incorporeal. Tertullian says that it means a material breath, which filled the body of Adam, became condensed, and assumed the shape of the body.[99]

But when we begin to scrutinize these statements of the Fathers, we find that the battle between the two camps is a sham battle, only a battle of words. On the one hand, we find that those Fathers who say the soul is incorporeal qualify the term incorporeal. They say that this term should not be taken in an absolute sense. God alone is incorporeal in the absolute sense of the term. The soul is incorporeal only in a relative sense: in relation to the body; it is not a body like the body with which it united.[100] On the other hand, we also find that Tertullian, who maintains that the soul is corporeal, qualifies the term corporeal. He says that the soul is corporeal in the sense that it is a "body of a quality and kind peculiar to itself (*propriae qualitatis et sui generis*),"[101] and not in the sense in which bodies are corporeal.

Since therefore the incorporeality of those who say that the soul is incorporeal only means that it is not corporeal like the body and since also the corporeality of Tertullian who says that the soul is corporeal does not mean that the soul is corporeal like the body, the difference between them is only verbal.

But how did they happen to come to such a verbal

[98] Gen. 2:7.
[99] *De Anima* 9.
[100] Cf., for instance. Irenaeus, *Adv. Haer.* V, 7, 1.
[101] *De Anima* 9.

difference? Here is the answer, in short. In Scripture, whether the Old or the New Testament, the term incorporeal does not occur—a fact already pointed out by Origen.[102] The scriptural equivalent for the philosophic "incorporeality" is "unlikeness." It was Philo who introduced into religious philosophy the term "incorporeal" as the equivalent of the term "unlike."[103] Now, if all the Fathers and also Tertullian were to describe the soul in scriptural terms, they would all describe it as being unlike the body. But since, as philosophers, they chose to use philosophic terms, most Fathers preferred the term incorporeal to express that unlikeness, whereas Tertullian preferred the term corporeal qualified by the expression *sui generis*.

Similarly with regard to the problem of the origin of the soul, we find that the Fathers are divided into different camps. In this case, there are three camps. In technical language, the views of these three camps are known as those of creation, pre-existence, and traducianism. In plain English, they may be described, respectively, as the theory of custom-made souls, the theory of ready-made souls, and the theory of second-hand souls.

According to the custom-made theory, at the birth of each child, God creates a soul especially for that child. According to the ready-made theory, at the time of the creation of the world, God in his foresight created individual souls which in number and variety were sufficient to supply the need of all the future generations of men. These souls are kept in a place the exact name of which is variously given by various authorities who are expert in the knowledge of these

---

[102] *De Princip.* I, Praef. 8.
[103] Cf. *Philo*, II, 94–100.

matters. At each child's birth a soul suitable to his body is placed within him—though, judging by the great number of misfit souls in the world, one may infer that mistakes frequently occur. According to the secondhand theory of the soul, God, at the time of the creation of the world, created only one soul, and that is the soul of Adam. All our souls are only slices of the worn-out soul of our first ancestor, which, without being thoroughly cleansed and destained, are cut down and made to fit our own peculiar bodies.

Here, we must confess, the difference is more than verbal. Still, insofar as the problem of the relation of soul to body is concerned, there is no difference between them. All these three views agree that the soul, whatever its origin, may be described in the language of Philo and Scripture as being in the body as in a "garment," as in a "house," as in a "temple," as in a "tabernacle."[104] In short, it has an existence apart from the body.

And so, when the Epicureans argued that the soul cannot be immortal because it is "corporeal" and because it is "born" with the body, the Fathers would answer as follows: However the nature of the soul is described by us, whether as corporeal or as incorporeal, and however the origin of the soul conceived of by us, whether as created with the body or as pre-existent or as inherited, the soul is unlike the body and is not an inseparable part of the body. It can therefore survive the body.

Another Epicurean argument against immortality is that a soul without a body can have no consciousness,

[104] Cf. my *Philosophy of the Church Fathers*, I 2nd ed., rev. (Cambridge, Mass., 1964), 366–369.

no knowledge, and no memory, for all consciousness and knowledge and memory are the result of sensation and sensation has its seat in body.[105] In raising this objection, Lucretius adds, evidently referring to the Stoic theory of regeneration, that even if our body should be regenerated, "it would not concern us at all, when once the remembrance of our former selves were snapped in twain."[106] This thus becomes an argument not only against immortality but also against resurrection. What good is resurrection without consciousness and knowledge and remembrance of our former selves! What is such a resurrection but a disinterment like that of the body of an Egyptian Pharaoh dug out of his tomb in a pyramid! And what are the glories promised to the risen saints but useless trinkets surrounding the mummified corpse of a Tutankhamen!

It is in anticipation of such an argument that the Fathers in their discussion of resurrection maintain that the resurrected body remembers its former life. Thus Fathers of different conceptions of resurrection, such as Irenaeus,[107] Origen,[108] Lactantius,[109] and Augustine[110] say explicitly that the resurrected dead will remember their former lives.

When we read these statements about the existence of memory in the resurrected bodies, it would seem that this assertion of memory is taken by the Fathers as a part of the mystery of resurrection. In Irenaeus there is no attempt at an explanation. But, when immediately before his statement that the souls of the

[105] Lucretius, III, 624ff., 830–842.
[106] Ibid. 846–851.
[107] Adv. Haer. II, 34, 1.
[108] De Princip. II, 10, 4.
[109] Div. Inst. VII, 23.
[110] De Civ. Dei XX, 22.

resurrected bodies "remember the deeds which they have done here"[111] he says of bodily resurrection in general that "God is not so poor or resourceless"[112] as not to be able to bring this about, it would seem that the existence of memory in the resurrected bodies, like resurrection itself, is due to the plenitude and resourcefulness of God. Moreover, when he indicates that sometimes the resurrected bodies not only remember the past but also possess the prophetic gift of knowing the future,[113] it may be inferred that memory in the resurrected bodies is a divine gift like that of prophecy. Origen, speaking of the punishment of the wicked in the hereafter and trying to explain how they could remember the evil doings of their past life, says that "the mind itself or conscience," which "by divine power" (per divinum virtutem) had received them "into memory" (in memoriam), "will see a kind of history, as it were, of all the foul and shameful and unholy deeds, which it has done, exposed before its eyes."[114] By the same token, we may reason, when Origen, speaking of the reward awaiting the saints in the hereafter, says that "they are to be instructed regarding all the things which they had seen on earth,"[115] so that "they may enjoy an unspeakable joy" by their acquisition "of full knowledge"[116] of those things which they had seen on earth, he means thereby that "the mind itself or conscience" had "by divine power" received those things "into memory." Lactantius, like Irenaeus, attempts no explanation. But in

---

[111] Adv. Haer. II, 34, 1.
[112] Ibid. II, 33, 5.
[113] Ibid. II, 34, 1.
[114] De Princip. II, 10, 4.
[115] Ibid. II, 11, 6 (ed. Koetschau, p. 190, 11, 4-5).
[116] Ibid. II, 11, 6 [5] (p. 189, 11, 9-13).

that very same passage, where he says of the resurrected
bodies that "they will remember their former life and
all its actions," he makes the following statement about
resurrection in general: "Let no one ask of us how this
is possible, for no reason can be assigned for divine
works (*divinorum operum*)."[117] To him, therefore,
memory in the resurrected bodies would be one of the
"divine works" for which "no reason can be assigned."
Augustine explains it as having been brought about "by
means of that indwelling of God in their . . . minds"
(*per hoc quod erat Deus . . . in eorum . . . mentibus*),
by which prophets were able to know things that had
not yet happened.[118] To him, therefore, the resurrected
saints will remember the past by an "indwelling of
God" like that by which prophets know the future—an
explanation which, as we have seen, is hinted at by
Irenaeus.

But this plenitude and resourcefulness of God or this
work of God or this divine power or this indwelling
of God by which the resurrected bodies are said by the
Fathers to possess memory of the past, we shall try to
show, is not part of what the Fathers consider the
mystery of resurrection but is rather a logical corollary
of their conception of the soul.

The conception of the soul common to all the
Fathers is essentially Platonic. The main characteristic
of that Platonic conception of the soul is its separability from the body. But, as to how that Platonic conception of the separability of the soul is to be understood,
there are two interpretations. According to one interpretation, in every human being, from his very birth,
there are two souls, one separable and one inseparable,

[117] *Div. Inst.* VII, 23.
[118] *De Civ. Dei* XX, 22.

and it is the inseparable soul in which memory, that is, memory of past sensations, originates. According to another interpretation, in every human being, at his birth, there is only one soul, a separable soul, and it is from this one separable soul, as a result of sensuous encrustments, that another soul is exuviated, which other soul becomes inseparably entangled with the body. Still it is in that original separable soul that the power of memory resides, even the power of memorizing the impressions and images of past sensations and, because memory originates and resides in that separable soul, it can be preserved in that soul even after it has become separated from the body.

This is a statement of the two contrasting interpretations of the Platonic conception of the separability of the soul presented simply without the obfuscation of technical terminology and without the incrustation of historical data as to origin and exponents. Suffice it to say that Philo represents the two-soul theory, and some Fathers, mainly unorthodox, follow him. Orthodox Fathers who are conscious of the implications of the problem follow, as a rule, the one-soul theory. It is also to be noted that both those who follow the two-soul theory and those who follow the one-soul theory support their view by the verse, "And the Lord God . . . breathed into his nostrils the breath of life,"[119] each side interpreting that verse in accordance with its own view. It is in this philosophic conception of one-soul that the Fathers find a philosophic rationalization for the attribution of memory to the resurrected dead. The plenitude and resourcefulness of God or the divine work or the divine power or the indwelling of God by which the Fathers mentioned above try to explain the

[119] Gen. 2:7.

possibility of memory in the resurrected bodies refers to that power of memory with which God has endowed the human soul and which that soul can retain even after its separation from the body. Thus also Plotinus, starting with a Platonic conception of soul, argues that the soul retains memories of its bodily life even after its separation from the body.[120]

And so, when the Epicureans argued that the immortal soul or the regenerated body can have no memory, because memory depends upon sensation and sensation depends upon body, and a body which has no interrupted existence, the Fathers would answer as follows: All this would indeed have to follow from the conception of soul held by your own school of thought. We, however, belong to another school of thought, a school of thought which claims discipleship of Plato, and according to this school of thought the soul itself is endowed with the power of memory, and it is the soul itself which remembers the past even when it is divested of its body during the state of its immortality, and it is also the soul itself which retains the memories of the past and in its state of existence when it is reclothed with its body at the time of its resurrection.

A third Epicurean argument against immortality is that the bodiless soul cannot experience any of the pleasures of life, for pleasure is based upon desire, and desire is based upon want, but a bodiless soul has no wants and hence no desire.[121] This argument, the Fathers must have felt, was also an argument against resurrection, inasmuch as the resurrected body, it is generally admitted by them, will not be subject to any

[120] *Enneades* IV, 3, 25ff.
[121] Lucretius, III, 894–901.

of the desires of the body and hence will not experience any of the pleasures of the body. Though the Fathers have proved to their own satisfaction that the body resurrected to eternal life will have memory, they still felt the force of the argument that, without a constant renewal of experience, eternal life would be a life without pleasure. It would be the life of an eternal paralytic, who sees all and knows all and remembers all, but experiences nothing pleasurable.

In anticipation of this argument, the Fathers try to show how it will be possible for the resurrected saints to experience a kind of pleasure which is not based upon want and desire. And ironically enough, the pleasure without want and desire, by the assumption of which the Fathers seek to refute the Epicurean denial of the possibility of pleasure in the immortal souls, is a concept borrowed from the Epicureans' own philosophy. It is that kind of pleasure which the Epicureans describe as "static pleasure" (καταστηματικὴ ἡδονή) or "joy worth mentioning" (ἀξιόλογος χαρά) or "the highest and surest joy" (ἡ ἀκροτάτη χαρὰ καὶ βεβαιοτάτη) and which, according to them, is not based upon want and desire but rather upon "freedom from mental disturbance" (ἀταραξία) and "freedom from bodily pain" (ἀπονία).[122] With this Epicurean "freedom from mental disturbance" (ἀταραξία) the Fathers sometimes combine the Stoic impassibility (ἀπάθεια), either because they regarded the differences that there may be between the Epicureans and the Stoics on this point as irrelevant for their own purposes or because they regarded these differences between the Epicureans and the Stoics as a mere battle of words. What was

122 Cf. C. Bailey, Epicurus, Fragmenta 1 (p. 120), LXXXI (p. 118), 11 (p. 122).

significant for the Fathers was the fact that to both the
Epicureans and the Stoics there was a kind of pleasure
which was not based upon want and desire, but was
purely of a negative nature, consisting in the absence
of something which causes the opposite of pleasure,
but yet, though negative, the mind was conscious and
aware of it.

It is this kind of pleasure, the Epicurean "static
pleasure" or "joy worth mentioning" or "the highest
and purest joy" consisting in that which the Epicureans
themselves describe as "freedom from mental disturbance" and "freedom from bodily pain" and in that
which the Stoic describes as "impassibility," that the
Fathers attribute to the resurrected saints. Tertullian,
commenting upon the verse, "eternal pleasure (*iocun-
ditas*) shall be upon their heads . . . and sorrow and
sighing shall flee away,"[123] takes the "eternal pleasure"
to refer to the pleasure to be experienced by the saints
after the resurrection, when "sorrow and sighing" will
cease by "the cessation of their causes, that is to say,
the afflictions of flesh and soul (*laesurae carnis atque
animae*)."[124] Now the "cessation of . . . the afflictions
of body and soul" is nothing but the Epicurean *aponia*
and *ataraxia*, that is to say, freedom from bodily pain
and mental disturbance. Thus, again, speaking of the
resurrected body, he says that, despite its being flesh
and endowed with all the sensation of flesh, it will be
"impassible" (*impassibilis*), inasmuch as it has been
liberated by the Lord for the very end and purpose of
being no longer capable of enduring suffering."[125]
Here, again, the term "impassible" is nothing but the

[123] Isa. 35:10.
[124] *De Resur. Carn.* 58.
[125] *Ibid.* 57.

Stoic ἀπαθής. Similarly Augustine, speaking of the eternal felicity of the saints in the city of God after the resurrection, says: "True peace shall be there, where no one shall suffer (*patietur* = πείσεται) opposition either from himself or from any other."[126] The term peace here reflects the term peace (εἰρήνη) which together with joy (χαρά) is promised by Paul to prevail in the Kingdom of God[127] and it is quite evidently taken by Augustine as the scriptural equivalent of the Epicurean *ataraxia* and *aponia* and the Stoic *apatheia*.

And so, when the Epicureans argued that an immortal soul or a regenerated body could experience no pleasure because pleasure is based upon desire and desire is based upon want, the Fathers would answer that the immortal souls and resurrected bodies will have exactly that kind of pleasure which the Epicureans themselves claim that man can have during his lifetime—a pleasure not based upon want and desire but one based upon freedom from both mental disturbance and bodily pain.

One of the essential characteristics of the Patristic conception of immortality and resurrection, as we have seen, is that they are acts of divine will. This, implying as it does that, if God willed, he could withhold them, implies also that, when God does will to bestow them upon man, he does so as a reward of righteousness. But any reward of God, as both the Old and the New Testament say, is rendered to "every man according to his work."[128] The Fathers, therefore, assume that there will be some difference in the rewards awaiting the

---

[126] *De Civ. Dei* XXII, 30.
[127] Rom. 14:17.
[128] Ps. 62:13(12); Matt. 16:27; cf. Eph. 6:8.

righteous after the resurrection of their bodies or also during the state of the immortality of their souls. The difference of reward is expressed by some Fathers, such as Irenaeus,[129] Clement of Alexandria,[130] and Augustine,[131] as a difference in the "mansions" in which the righteous will abide, basing their view upon the verse, "In my Father's house are many mansions."[132] Though we are not told in the New Testament how many mansions there will be, Irenaeus and Clement of Alexandria supply us with the needed information. They tell us that there will be three such mansions, and in proof of this they quote from the parable of the sower the following verse: "But others fell into good ground and brought forth fruit, some an hundredfold, some sixtyfold, some thirtyfold."[133] These three mansions, or abiding places of the righteous, are described by Irenaeus as "the heavens" ($o\dot{v}\rho\alpha\nu o\acute{\iota}$), "paradise" ($\pi\alpha\rho\acute{\alpha}\delta\epsilon\iota\sigma os$) and "the city" ($\pi\acute{o}\lambda\iota s$).[134] In the New Testament, it may be remarked, while these three terms occur as designations of the future abode of the righteous, there is no evidence that they are meant to designate three different places. Clement of Alexandria does not designate the three mansions by special names. He only says: "There are various mansions, according to the worth of those who have believed." The highest of these mansions, however, is described by him as that "where the Lord is."[135] It is interesting to note that Philo, who speaks only of immortality,

[129] Adv. Haer. V, 36, 2.
[130] Stromata VI, 14.114 (PG 9, 337B).
[131] In Joannis Evangelium LXVII, 14, 2; De Virginitate 26.
[132] John 14:2.
[133] Matt. 13:8.
[134] Adv. Haer. V, 36, 1.
[135] Stromata VI, 14.114 (PG 9, 337B).

but describes immortality in terms of resurrection,[136] similarly enumerates three places where the immortal souls abide. He describes these three abiding-places as follows: (1) heaven, the place of the angels; (2) the intelligible world, the place of the ideas; (3) above the intelligible world of ideas, described by him as the place where those who are immortal are stationed by God "near himself."[137] Clement's place "where the Lord is" would seem to correspond to Philo's place "near [God] himself." This is also, we may assume, what Irenaeus means when he describes the highest mansion as "the city," for the three mansions are described by him as the places where "God[138] [or the Lord Savior[139]] shall be seen according as they who see him shall be worthy,"[140] and consequently the highest mansion or "the city" is the place which, in the language of Clement, is "where the Lord is" and, in the language of Philo, is "near [God] himself," that is to say, the place where the most righteous will have the highest vision of God.

The differences in the reward of the righteous are thus, as says Irenaeus, differences in their vision of God or in what is generally known as the beatific vision. Though the promise of the vision of God or the beatific vision is based upon scriptural texts, such as "They shall see God";[141] "For now we see him in a

---

[136] Cf. Philo I, 404–06.
[137] Sacr. 3, 8; cf. Philo I, 403–404.
[138] So in the Latin version.
[139] So in the Greek fragment. See comment ad loc. in W. W. Harvey's edition of Irenaeus' Adversus Haereses (Vol. II, 428, n. 2).
[140] Adv. Haer. V, 36, 1 end.
[141] Matt. 5:8.

mirror darkly, but then face to face";[142] "We shall be like him, for we shall see him as he is,"[143] it is treated by the Fathers philosophically, taken by them to refer to a direct knowledge of God in contradistinction to a knowledge of him indirectly through his work in the world.[144] The vision of God or the beatific vision thus reflects what Plato calls the vision of the ideas,[145] what Philo calls the vision of God,[146] and what Plotinus calls the vision of the One,[147] except that with the Fathers this immediate knowledge of God is reserved for the saints in their immortal or resurrected state.

Immortality and resurrection are sometimes described as salvation, though salvation in Christianity has a wider meaning than resurrection. The question may therefore be raised whether such salvation is confined only to those who believed in Christ or whether others who do not believe in Christ, especially Jews who follow the Law and pagans who, through philosophy gave up the worship of idols and lead a virtuous life, may also attain salvation.

The question is raised by the very first philosophic Church Father, Justin Martyr, in his *Dialogue with Trypho.*

Justin himself is represented there as a convert to Christianity who before his conversion was a Platonic philosopher and had given up the worship of idols and led an upright life. Trypho is represented as a Jew who has a vague and faulty knowledge of Christianity. He

---

[142] I Cor. 13:12.
[143] I John 3:2.
[144] Cf., for instance, Augustine, *De Civ. Dei* XXII, 29.
[145] *Republic* VII, 532 A–C.
[146] Cf. Philo II, 83ff.
[147] *Enneades* II, 9, 15; V, 5, 6; VI, 7, 31.

looks upon Christianity as a form of idolatry, the worship of a human being as God, and accordingly he regards Justin's conversion to Christianity as a relapse from a philosophic veneration of God to idol worship. He, therefore, says to Justin: "It would be better for you to follow Plato or any other philosopher . . . for, whilst you remained in that mode of philosophy and lived blamelessly (ἀμέμπτως), a hope for better destiny were left for you. But now that you have deserted God and placed your hope on a man, what means of salvation were left for you?"[148]

This statement of Trypho that, if Justin had remained a philosopher who had given up idolatry and led a blameless life, he would have had hope for a better destiny reflects a view which was common at that time among Jews, Hellenistic as well as Palistinian. In Philo it is expressed in his statements where he speaks of those among Greeks "who practice wisdom and live blamelessly (ἀνεπιλήπτως) and irreproachably (ἀνυπαιτίως)"[149] and where he applies the terms "wise and just and virtuous" not only to the Jewish Essenes but also to the seven wise men of Greece, the Magi among the Persians, and the Gymnosophists in India,[150] all of whom are regarded by him as what may be described as spiritual proselytes.[151] Palestinian Judaism expresses itself on this point in the Tannaitic saying that "pious gentiles have a portion in the world to come."[152]

[148] *Dial.* 8.
[149] *Spec.* II, 12, 44.
[150] *Probus* 11, 72–75.
[151] Cf. Philo, II, 372–374.
[152] *Tos. Sanhedrin* XIII, 2.

In his answer, Justin maintains that, after the advent of Christ, salvation can come only through Christ,[153] which thus excludes both Jews and gentile philosophers who do not believe in Christ. The same view is held by Clement of Alexandria, who maintains that Jews can be saved only by confessing faith in Jesus and pagan philosophers can be saved only by both abandoning idolatry and confessing faith in Jesus.[154] Augustine reaffirms this view succinctly in his statement that "outside the true Church everything is possible except salvation (*extra ecclesiam catholicam totum potest praeter salutem*)"[155] and, when the Pelagians were reported to him as believing that "the Law leads to the kingdom of heaven,"[156] he exclaimed that while they "are not Jews in name, they become so by their error."[157]

With regard to those, however, who lived before the advent of Christ, Justin Martyr declares that the righteous men in the Old Testament before Moses and those who were righteous under the Law after Moses, but before Christ, will be saved by Christ in his second coming.[158] Evidently this would exclude pre-Christian pagan philosophers, seeing that whatever righteousness they may have had was not the kind of righteousness described by Justin as being "under the Law." In contradistinction to this, however, the mysterious author known as The Ambrosiaster, in his comment on the

---

[153] *Dial.* 26.
[154] *Stromata* VI, 6.44.4 (PG 9, 205B); VI, 6.45.5-6 (PG 9, 268B).
[155] *Sermo ad Caesareensis Ecclesiae Plebem* 6 (PL 43, 695).
[156] *De Gestis Pelagii* 33; cf. *Epist.* 96, 1, 7.
[157] *Epistolae* 96, 1, 7.
[158] *Dial.* 44.

words "Nevertheless death reigned from Adam to Moses,"[159] says that over "those who have known God, either by tradition or by natural discovery, and have honored him, imparting the honor due to his name to nobody else . . . death did not reign . . . for it reigned only over those who worshipped the devil under the form of idols."[160] According to The Ambrosiaster, then, pre-Christian pagan philosophers who had given up idolatry were entitled to salvation. But this mysterious author, it has been conjectured, was either a native-born Jew who was first converted to Christianity and then reverted to Judaism or a native-born Christian[161] whose mind may have been perverted by his unusual fund of knowledge of Judaism and of Jewish literature which he displays in his writings. In either case, he may be regarded as having subverted an old established Christian view. No wonder then, when in the fourteenth century the question was raised whether Aristotle would be saved, the answer was in the negative and, when later, in the fifteenth century, an attempt was made to answer in the affirmative, general opinion was against it.[162]

In their attempt to cite philosophic testimonial and analogies for immortality and resurrection,[163] the pur-

[159] Rom. 5:14.

[160] In Epistolam ad Romanos V, 14 (PL 17, 99B).

[161] G. Morin, "L'Ambrosiaster et le Juif Converti Isaac, Contemporain du Pape Damase," Revue d'Histoire et de Littérature Religieuses 4 (1899), 97–121; id., "Hilarius L'Ambrosiaster," Revue Bénédictine 20 (1903), 113–131.

[162] Cf. A. H. Chroust, "A Contribution to the Mediaeval Discussion: Utrum Aristotelis sit Salvatus," Journal of the History of Ideas 6 (1945), 231–238.

[163] I have not dealt here with the analogies of resurrection drawn by the Fathers from the various natural phenomena of the vanishing and reappearance of things.

pose of the Fathers, as we have seen, was not to explain why they believed in this twofold doctrine, but rather to show, on the basis of those philosophic testimonials and analogies, that it was not logically absurd. To the Fathers, the real basis of this twofold doctrine was scripture and tradition, and the main argument for its not being logically absurd was that it belonged to the miraculous acts of God; and miraculous acts of God, within the Father's own system of thought, were not inconsistent with reason, for such acts were to be explained on the general principle that all things are possible to God. Both Justin Martyr[164] and Tertullian[165] clinch their defense of the doctrine of resurrection by quoting the verse, "The things which are impossible with men are possible with God"[166] and Celsus reports that Christians defend their belief in resurrection by a paraphrase of that New Testament verse to the effect that "everything is possible to God."[167] Origen, in his reply to Celsus, does not deny the miraculous nature of resurrection as an act of the divine will[168] nor does he deny the defense thereof on the ground that "everything is possible to God"; what he does is only to qualify the term "everything" by excluding things that are "nonexistent" (τὰ ἀνύπαρκτα) or "inconceivable" (τὰ ἀδιανόητα) or "disgraceful" (αἰσχρά),[169] and to maintain that resurrection, especially as he understood it, is neither anything nonexistent nor anything inconceivable nor anything disgraceful.

[164] Apologia I, 19.
[165] De Resur. Carn. 57.
[166] Luke 18:27; cf. Matt. 19:26.
[167] Cont. Cels. V, 14.
[168] Ibid. V, 22.
[169] Ibid. V, 23.

This belief that everything is possible to God, traceable, of course, to the Old Testament teaching expressed in the verse, which in the Septuagint reads, "I know that thou canst do all things, and that to thee nothing is impossible,"[170] is exactly the principle by which Philo justifies the miraculous power of God to change the laws of nature which he himself has implanted in the world.[171] No less than in four places in his writings does he repeat the statement that "all things are possible to God"[172] and in one of these places, almost in the words quoted from the New Testament, his statement reads: "The things which are impossible to every created being are possible to him alone."[173] Indeed the Stoic Chrysippus, as quoted by Lactantius, in speaking of this theory of palingenesis or cycles, says: "But since this is so, it is evident that nothing is impossible (οὐδὲν ἀδύνατον), and that we, after our death, when certain periods of time have again come round, are restored to this state in which we are now."[174] This universal negative proposition, "nothing is impossible," which is inferred by Chrysippus from the Stoic palingenesis and which logically amounts to the same as the universal affirmative proposition, "all things are possible," would at first sight seem to have the same meaning as the scriptural proposition "all things are possible to God" by which the Fathers justify their belief in resurrection. However, it has not the same meaning. What Chrysippus means

[170] Job 42:2.
[171] Cf. Philo, I, 325–356.
[172] Opif. 14, 46; Jos. 40, 244; Mos. I, 31, 174; Qu. in Gen. IV, 17.
[173] Mos. I, 31, 174.
[174] Div. Inst. VII, 23.

by his "nothing is impossible" is that nothing in the eternal succession of the generation and destruction of the world, with the eternal succession of the birth and death of every individual human being within the world, is to be thought of as impossible or can be rendered impossible, for these cycles in the world's course are predetermined by fate or necessity or nature. It does not mean that it is possible for anything to happen which has not been predetermined by the eternal and necessary order of nature, for, as says Chrysippus, in a passage quoted by Plutarch, "No particular thing, not even the least, can be otherwise than according to common nature and its reason," to which Plutarch adds that by "common nature and its reason" Chrysippus means "fate."[175] To the Fathers, however, the scriptural principle that "all things are possible to God" means that God can change the laws of nature which he himself has implanted in the world, and resurrection is such a change in the laws of nature, whence it is not an act of nature but an act of divine will.

Plato, to whom immortality was natural to the soul, said that "immortality is in us."[176] Reflecting this sentiment and restating it in terms of his own belief that immortality together with resurrection is a gift of God, Gregory of Nyssa says that since one of the attributes of God is eternal existence, it was needful that we, who were created in the image of God, should not be without the "gift of this attribute" but that our nature "should have in itself the immortal" and that it should

175 Arnim, S. V. F., II, 937.
176 Laws IV, 713 E.

"be possessed with a desire for divine and eternal life."[177] Augustine repeats this sentiment when he says that "we are conscious in ourselves of having a desire" for eternal life,[178] and he finds an intimation of this in Paul's statement that we are "earnestly desiring to be clothed upon with our house which is from heaven."[179]

With such a desire, I imagine we are all still possessed, and we should, therefore, quite naturally like to know what meaning for us today have these views of the Fathers on immortality and resurrection— especially for those of us today who think that we need a new kind of promise and a new kind of hope for a new kind of fulfillment of this our innate desire and longing for eternal life.

This kind of knowledge, I regret to say, I cannot supply. I am the dragoman of the Fathers; I am not their neo-izer. As one who for the past hour has acted the part of pure historian, I should not like to perform before your very eyes a feat of quick-change artistry and of a sudden turn myself into theologian and preacher, and that kind of theologian and preacher, too, who would make the Fathers talk latter-day beliefs and latter-day disbeliefs in the pious language of their own old beliefs. But I think I shall not be stepping out of my character as historian if I let the Fathers speak for themselves.

Let us then imagine that the Fathers are with us here now in body, as I hope they are with us in spirit. Let us further imagine that a bright young man, a student of divinity, came up to tell them how sorry he was that he could not share with them their belief

---

[177] *Oratio Catechetica Magna* 5 (PG 45, 21D).
[178] *De Peccatorum Meritis et Remissione* I, 2, 2.
[179] II Cor. 5:2.

in the resurrection of the body, seeing that modern science is all against its possibility, but how glad he was that he could share with them their belief in the immortality of the soul, seeing that respectable modern philosophers and even respectable modern scientists with a philosophic turn of mind do occasionally give a nod of approval to immortality.

To this, I imagine, the Fathers would answer:

Young man, you are wrong on two counts.

You are wrong, first, in blaming your unwillingness to believe in resurrection upon modern science. The impossibility of resurrection and the fact of its being contrary to what is known as the laws of nature had already been proclaimed by the outmoded ancient science of our own time; modern science of your present time cannot make it more impossible. Still, if we, despite the science of our time, were willing to believe in resurrection and you, because of the science of your time, are unwilling to believe in it, your unwillingness to believe in it is not to be explained by the opposition of the science of your time. It is to be explained on other grounds, and there are other grounds by which it can be explained.

You are wrong, second, in distinguishing between immortality and resurrection, by assuming the former to be scientifically possible and the latter scientifically impossible. The kind of immortality in which we believe, immortality by the will of God, and even the kind of immortality in which Plato believed, immortality by nature, is discarded by science—by the modern science of your time—just as is resurrection. The immortality which respectable philosophers and even respectable scientists with a philosophic turn of mind sometimes speak of approvingly is another kind of immortality; it is the Aristotelian conception of immortality, a spurious sort of immortality, an immortality not by the will of God nor by the necessity of nature but by the word of man. And let us tell you the story of Aristotle. He started as a disciple of Plato, with the belief that the soul, or rather one of the souls or one part of the soul, is separable from the body and is immortal. His works still contain reminiscences of this early belief of his, as when, for instance, he says of the intelligent part of the soul (νοῦς) that it may survive after death[180] or that it is immortal and eternal.[181] But when later he found himself forced, by reason of his revised conception of soul, to deny the immortality of any part of the human soul, he held out as a consolation the immortality of the human race. Man as individual indeed dies, but the human race, of which the individual man is part, lives on forever.[182]

And here the Fathers would make their final remark: Dear young man, if you can find consolation in this verbal kind of immortality and if this verbal kind of immortality can serve you as an incentive to do good and shun evil, go and console yourself and sin no more, and mayhap the Lord in his mercy will reward you with true immortality, aye, and with resurrection, too.

And to this, and with this, we say, Amen.[183]

[180] *Metaphysica* XII, 3, 1070a, 24–26.
[181] *De Anima* III, 5, 430a, 23.
[182] *Ibid.* II, 4, 415b, 6–7.
[183] EDITOR'S NOTE: When Professor Wolfson's Ingersoll Lecture appeared in his collected essays *Religious Philosophy* (Belknap Press, 1961), it was discussed in some detail by diverse reviewers. In 1964 Professor Wolfson gave a rather extensive answer to some of these critics in an article entitled "Notes on Patristic Philosophy," *Harvard Theological Review*, 57 (1964), pp. 119–31.

THE GREEK IDEAS
OF IMMORTALITY

THE INGERSOLL LECTURE FOR 1958

Werner Jaeger

THE Immortality of Man was one of the fundamental creeds of the philosophical religion of Platonism that was in part adopted by the Christian church and that thus became one of the foundations of the Christian civilization of the Eastern and Western world. Ever since Paul in the fifteenth chapter of I Corinthians made resurrection the cornerstone of the Christian faith the church has had a profound interest in the ancient philosophers who taught that man's soul is immortal and does not perish along with its mortal companion the body. Although this belief in the immortality of the soul, the ψυχή, is not the same as the Christian idea of man's resurrection in the flesh or in a transfigured body, both religious ideas have a natural affinity with each other; and it is therefore easy to understand that the Platonic belief in immortality was regarded as an anticipation of the Christian resurrection and helpful to the faithful who might wish to check their emotional expectations of a future life after death by rational reflection. Thus we find attempts to compare both things or to look for natural phenomena that could be interpreted as analogies of resurrection in nature. In his letter to the Corinthians Clement of Rome referred to the mythical bird Phoenix, which is reborn and rises from the ashes periodically, and he thereby created a symbol that has proved unbelievably fruitful in the millennial tradition of Christian poetry and religious thought. It took some time for the Christian authors of the ancient period to distinguish sharply between the pagan concept of immortality and the Christian idea of resurrection, and some of them contaminated the two unhesitatingly. In Gregory of Nyssa's famous dialogue *De anima et resurrectione*, written after the death of his sister Saint Macrina and recording his last conversation with her before she died, we find this typical fusion of pagan and Christian ideas expressed in the very title of the book, which contains them both.

In some of the previous Ingersoll Lectures I have found references to a different kind of immortality than the survival of the human person after death. Such are man's physical survival in his offspring, or his social survival in the honor shown him by the community in keeping his name and memory alive after his death. This form of belief was by some of the lecturers regarded as a kind of modern substitute or *Ersatz* for the genuine belief in personal immortality, and they therefore dismissed it from serious consideration. Since we are concerned today with the special forms the idea of immortality took among the ancient Greeks, we must observe that it is exactly this approach to the problem of life and death that is found originally in Greek tradition, whereas belief in the immortality of the soul is a later product of the Greek mind. It cannot be separated from the development of the idea of the soul, which is itself an important stage in the history of Greek thought and should not be taken for granted. It is one thing to be a Christian who believes in resurrection and to look back upon this later stage of Greek

culture in order to find confirmation of my faith in
Plato or other pagan philosophers; and it is quite another thing to be a historian of the Greek mind who
tries to grasp the rhythm of its evolution and present
it in its various stages, including its final merger with
the Christian religion. Since the latter is my natural
methodical approach to the problem, I hope you will
permit me to start with the earlier phase, which we
find reflected in the oldest Greek poetry, Homer and
his successors, and ascend from there to the ideas of a
later spiritual philosophy of the human soul, Plato and
his followers.

In the early poetic tradition there is a sharp cleavage
between men and gods. Men are called mortals, and
it is the distinctive mark of the gods that they are
immortal. The specific words for man (ἀνήρ or
ἄνθρωπος) are used mostly in contrast to the gods.
Indeed, we look in vain in the Homeric epics, the Iliad
and the Odyssey, for the view that men survive their
bodies. The Trojan war sent to Hades the ψυχαί of
many heroes, whereas "they themselves" were thrown
to dogs and birds of prey. "They themselves" means
their bodies; thus some modern interpreters have concluded that the ψυχή that goes to the underworld must
be something like the soul, especially since "soul" is the
later meaning of the word ψυχή. But Homer describes
ψυχαί of the dead as mere shadows without conscious
life or mental activity. They lost all memory of life
when they crossed the stream of Lethe, the river of
forgetfulness. Homer calls them "idols," a kind of
ghosts, resembling their former shape and face, but
there is no passage in Homer where ψυχή is used of a
living man and means what we call a soul. For that
he uses other words, which are mostly taken from parts

of the body such as the heart or the diaphragm, or from affections of the body such as the heat of anger (θυμός, Latin *fumus*). The ψυχή leaves the body with the last breath; originally, therefore, the word ψυχή, which comes from ψύχειν (to breathe), must have had something to do with the breath of life, just like the Latin *anima* and *animus*, which are etymologically related to the Greek word for wind, ἄνεμος; but in Homer ψυχή is no longer the breath and even less the conscious soul with all its functions. The only thing that survives a man's physical existence is his name, which is kept alive by his fame. This seems to make it certain that there was a difference between the great mass of mortals who had nothing to hope for after death and the valiant and noble warriors who left behind them the glorious memory of their deeds to live on in the songs of the ἀοιδοί. In these songs the great deeds of gods and men were equally praised; the difference between mortals and immortals seemed almost to disappear, and man acquired eternal glory and reputation. His personality was strong enough to resist the common law of oblivion. Professor Clark said something similar about the Indian religion, and Kittredge described that of the old Germanic tribes in colors that remind one of the Greeks in their heroic age. But Homer knows no Walhall. Poetry is man's immortality, as it were, for it is essentially praise, as Homer, Hesiod, and their successors tell us explicitly; and the strongest motive for the greatest heroic effort of an individual is that it will make him survive in song so as to be known to future generations (καὶ ἐσσομένοισι πυθέσθαι).

The first time that we are told expressly that a man will become "immortal" (ἀθάνατος) is therefore quite logically in martial poetry. This is in one of the few elegies preserved of the Spartan Tyrtaeus (seventh century), who promises this as their future lot to the valiant warriors who have died for their country. The new thing here is that the country, the community of the *polis*, takes over, as it were, the function of the Homeric singer who praises the virtue of his heroes. In the new phase of Greek life embodied in the city or *polis*, the community guarantees eternal memory to those who have given their lives for it. Tyrtaeus says: the hero, although he is under the earth, nevertheless becomes immortal. In other words, where the idea of immortality occurs for the first time it is meant as a great paradox. In the cult religion of the Greek city the heroes of old who are interred in the tombs, the θῆκαι, are always mentioned along with the upper gods (θεοὶ ὕπατοι), and the new heroes who have died in battle enjoy similar honors: they receive public burial and a tomb revered by all, young and old, and their name survives both in the memory of the living community and in the songs of men at their symposia. The individual is socialized as a member of the *polis*, but, in an ideal sense, he maintains and forever preserves his individuality by giving up his life to the community. It is not accidental that the question of his immortality is raised at this moment. Obviously this belief in his immortality is more than a poetic metaphor, for it assures him of the imperishable value of his personality, which is invested in his name and fame. There is one great difference between this idea of glory, which I would like to call its political form, and the glory of the Homeric heroes; and that is that the *aretē* of the individual citizen of a Greek *polis* is measured by its relation to the common good.

In a way this kind of immortality, which appears so

natural in the early Greek community of the *polis,*
never died as long as the Greek *polis* was alive. It is still
invoked by the orators of the Athenian democracy of
the fifth and fourth centuries in their patriotic funeral
speeches delivered at the graves of the soldiers who
have died in the great wars for the liberty of the land,
such as Pericles' funeral oration or that in Plato's
Menexenus. It is the *polis* of Athens that bestows
immortality on them, and they need no Homer. In
Plato's Symposium we notice a characteristic change:
the warrior is no longer the only one who is entitled to
this immortality. Other men of fame share his honor:
the lawgiver, the poet, the writer, the scientist, and the
philosopher. But they have this in common with the
old warrior immortality, that they are immortalized by
what they have achieved for the whole human community, not by their mere talent or genius. They are
animated by an insatiable *erōs,* like the physical *erōs*
that impels ordinary mortals to propagate their own
person and life in their offspring: in the same way the
great creative men of humanity are filled with a hunger
and thirst for achieving immortality by virtue of imperishable works. The physical and the spiritual *erōs*
spring from the same root, though they try to achieve
their objective on different levels. Thus we see the idea
of immortality take a more and more important place
in the human consciousness of the fourth century B.C.;
but even though the idea of the political community
and the common good is still the value to which every
form of human activity is related and which determines
a person's value, it seems evident that this original
authority of the social order is vanishing in real life and
that the highly differentiated individual of this century
is struggling hard to maintain a value of his own that

is independent of the great mass of men because it is rooted in something of eternal validity and in the depth of the human soul. We therefore expect, at this point of historical evolution, to encounter a new conception of immortality, the immortality of the soul. Indeed, the same Plato who interprets the creative effort of the human mind as the innate metaphysical erōs for immortal life, takes the step of declaring the soul itself immortal.

But where does this concept of soul have its origin in the history of the Greek mind, since we did not find any trace of it in Homer or in the earlier writers? Plato certainly did not create it single-handed; it had a previous development of its own, which, so far as we can trace it, takes us back to the sixth century B.C. In this period of social revolution and intellectual upheaval there is more than one group that seems to have contributed to the new conception of man's internal life and nature. The Orphic religion, the Pythagorean ideal of an ascetic life, and the religion of the so-called mysteries have this in common as against the cult religion of the great mass of the people, that they are concerned with man's inner life, however material its symbolic representation. They all think of man as being much closer to the divine than was commonly assumed, even as being himself of divine origin. In these circles we find for the first time the belief in the soul of man as something different and separable from the body. Unfortunately we know very little of these sects or of the cult of the mysteries, which were kept secret by the members, and we must therefore try to form an idea of them from sources that are considerably later than the sixth century. The Orphic religion, the origin of which was attributed to the mythical person of

Orpheus, the singer, was a βίος or way of life to keep
the soul pure and immaculate during its habitation in
the body, in order to enable it to return to its divine
home after death. Some speak of the body as the soul's
prison or tomb—σῶμα σῆμα, as the old formula quoted
by Plato has it. Pindar, who encountered the Orphic
religion in Sicily, in his second Olympian ode describes
the religious faith of its followers and their expectation
of a life after death: "Day and night the sun shines
for the guiltless in the world beyond, they do not
disquiet the earth with the strength of their hands,
neither the water of the sea, but among the honored
gods they enjoy a life without tears; while the wicked
suffer pain the sight of which none can bear; but those
who have kept their soul free from unjust deeds and
have maintained an innocent state for the space of
three lifetimes both here and beyond, they will walk
the path of Zeus to Kronos' tower. There the ocean
breezes sweep across the Island of the Blessed. Flowers
of gold flame from the radiant trees on the mainland,
while the water nourishes others, and with garlands of
these the blessed decorate themselves. . . ." Here we
have the concept of soul in a quite un-Homeric sense,
not as a shadow or idol in Hades, but living through
three lives in both worlds, here and beyond, and this
soul is the real subject of man's inner life. More descriptions of the soul's blessed life in the world beyond are
to be found in the preserved fragments of a Pindaric
θρῆνος, i.e., lament for somebody's death; but more
important than these colorful pictures of eternal bliss
is what is said there about the nature of the soul itself.
"The body of all men is subject to all-powerful death,
but there still remains alive an image of man's life, for
this alone comes from the gods. It sleeps when the

limbs are active, but to those that sleep, it presages in many a dream the decision of things delightful or doleful." Erwin Rohde, the author of the famous book *Psyche*, thought he should identify the εἴδωλον of this Pindaric passage with the Homeric idol in Hades; but the ghostlike ψυχή in Homer is never referred to while man is alive, but only when he dies or is dead in the sense of Pindar's description. More recent scholarship, however, has shown that we have here two entirely different conceptions of the ψυχή, the Homeric and the Orphic. The former is not a soul at all in our sense but a ghostlike shadow, whereas the Orphic conception presupposes not only a soul in the later sense of the word but its continuing existence, both while still imprisoned in the body and after its release from it. But it is not identical with the conscious life of man; we might call it the dream soul, because it is only in his dreams that man has any indication of its existence within himself. It is this independent existence of the dream soul inside us and its intensified activity in the face of death that makes Pindar (or the people whose faith he describes) believe in its continued existence after death. The idea of a migration of the soul, though not through beings other than human, is implied in Pindar's eschatology. On the other hand, this idea of soul is not based upon a physiological conclusion, but the soul becomes for the Orphic faith the hero of a moral drama that runs through three lives and ends either in its liberation and eternal rest among the gods or in eternal suffering—we would say, in heaven or hell. The idea of another Zeus who sits in judgment of the dead in Hades occurs also in Aeschylus' Suppliants, where it seems to be derived from Orphic sources.

Pindar is the fifth-century poet who apparently was

most fascinated by the eschatological myth of the
Orphic religion, although Wilamowitz may be correct
in saying that we have no right to conclude from his
picture in the second Olympian and in the Threnos
that Pindar was a convert himself. We find another
witness of that Orphic view in the epic poem of
Empedocles of Agrigentum (middle of the fifth century), which bore the significant title *Purifications*.
This same man also wrote a famous didactic poem on
the nature of the universe in which he appears as a
scientist and philosopher of nature thinking along the
line of strict material causality. It has been a matter
of speculation among scholars how he was able to
reconcile in himself both ways of thinking. Man belongs to both spheres of reality, the world of the cease-
less cycle of the physical elements, which attract each
other by love and repel each other by hatred, and the
world from which the soul of man arose before it was
wrapped in the strange garment of flesh. It is of divine
origin, and Empedocles calls it the daemon that dwells
upon this earth in exile from God. It lives in all sorts
of bodies through which it has to go on its endless
migration. We shudder when we read a thought like
this: "I too was once a boy and a girl, a bush and a
mute fish rising from the depths of the sea." Empedocles seems to embrace all these forms of life with
melancholy sympathy. His is the understanding love of
one who feels their existence from within, and none of
them is more remote from him than he is from himself.
From the unspeakable bliss of its heavenly home the
soul came down to the confinement of this cave, and
he remembers the moment: "I wept and wailed when
I caught sight of this unfamiliar place." So the immortality of the soul is linked by Empedocles with its pre-

existence and transmigration into other beings. This does not separate him from other than human creatures but makes him feel a profound solidarity with them. Hence he adopts the Orphic vegetarianism and strictly forbids the killing of animals. Empedocles is a special case among the so-called pre-Socratic thinkers because of his Orphism, but the belief in the divinity of the soul remains a problem also for other contemporaries, such as Diogenes of Apollonia, who follows in the footsteps of the earlier philosophers of nature and derives everything from one primal ground, but explains by his basic principle, which is the air, the origin of body and soul alike. The soul that animates the body is called by him "a small part of God," for it is a modification of the divine air and returns to its ethereal origin when it is separated from its body in death, whereas the material remains of the dead man return to earth. We see the problem of the soul's immortality here treated as a part of a pantheistic natural theology. This was the form in which it seems to have appealed to the sceptical mind of a Euripides, who reflects so often in his dramas the most enlightened thought of his time. The Orphic faith and the Dionysus mysteries also appear in his Hippolytus and in his Bacchae, but they interest him more as psychopathological phenomena. Nevertheless they are symptoms of a new approach to reality, of which Plato is our main witness: the immaterial world, which is his discovery, is the world of the soul, and it is the very center of Plato's thought.

There can be little doubt that Plato did not inherit his belief in the immortality of the soul from his master Socrates. In his Apology of Socrates we find a very reserved attitude towards the question of man's survival. Socrates considers it as perfectly possible that death is the end of man's existence. The opposite possibility, too, is discussed, and Socrates ironically anticipates the pleasure of this chance of continuing in the world beyond his favorite activity of questioning people, for which he was sentenced to death in this. But his "care for the soul," of which he speaks so frequently as his god-sent task, makes the soul appear as the greatest value in human life, its *aretē* as man's only source of true happiness. We witness in Plato's Socratic dialogues the birth of a new religion. Philosophy is for him a way of life that leads to the salvation ($\sigma\omega\tau\eta\rho\iota\alpha$) of the soul. In the Phaedo this faith stands the test in the hour of Socrates' death. Master and disciples are talking in the prison about the soul, its nature and destiny. Plato has arrived at the conviction that the soul is indestructible, and he lends this faith to the dying Socrates, since this unshakable confidence is the root of his life. His triumph over injustice is as complete as his victory over "fear and trembling." The scene is surrounded by peace and serenity. In this supreme hour the soul is preparing to separate itself from the body and the material world, as far as this can be done while it is still in the flesh, and it turns to the world of being that is the home of the philosopher.

Plato's conception of the soul is the crown of his philosophy of knowledge, and it could not have taken such definite shape without his theory of ideas. If we understand him correctly, this is what he tells us himself in his Phaedo, where he declares that the belief in the immortality of the soul stands or falls with this theory. The more he came to visualize the ideas as the only true being beyond the world of sense-perception, which Heraclitus had in mind when he said that everything is in perpetual flux, the more Plato was led to believe that the knowledge of the ideas, which springs from the soul itself and not from our senses, exists in the soul because it remembers what it once knew in a former life. This way of thinking was suggested to him not by Socrates but by the old Orphic myth about the origin and migration of the soul through several lives, and he expressly mentions the old formula σῶμα σῆμα, which for him takes on a new meaning. The way in which he makes use of various elements of Orphic eschatology in his myths about the destiny of the soul after death at the end of his Gorgias, Phaedo, and Republic proves unmistakably that he found truth in them if taken in a nonliteral sense. Of course the adept of the Orphic religion took these myths quite literally, but for Plato they have a different function: they present in mythical form a truth that Plato has tried to arrive at by way of dialectical inquiry. Nothing could be more wrong than to make Plato an Orphic, as some historians of religion and especially some students of Orphism in ancient Greece, such as Machioro, have tried to do, thereby making the problem simply one of good old-fashioned *Quellenforschung*. One might as well contend that Goethe became a Catholic at the end of the second part of Faust, since he there makes use of elements of Catholic religious symbolism for his poetic vision of heaven. Green philosophers often did this in order to create for themselves a philosophical language and a world of symbols analogous to those of religion, most of all Plato, who is great at this art. It is only natural that such symbolic analogies should not as a rule have been borrowed from the cult religion of the people but almost exclusively from the religion of the mystery cults or the Orphic sect, first, because theirs was a form of religion that consisted of symbolism, and second, because it was concerned with the individual man's salvation and hope for a better life after death. But the path leading to the happiness of the philosophical soul was different from that of the initiates of the Orphic sect. Their purification was through abstinence from certain things such as the flesh of animals or through a prescribed ritual; but the κάθαρσις of which we read in Plato's Phaedo is effected through the gradual ascent of the soul to the world of being by the long and toilsome way of knowledge. The Symposium gives an even more detailed picture of this ascent through knowledge, comparing it to the initiation in the successive stages of the mysteries. The soul thereby becomes more and more similar to the object of its knowledge, and only by this process of gradual assimilation to pure being and to the divine good can the knowledge of it finally be attained. Plato's language, his symbols, and his thoughts about the soul and its cosmic destiny are taken from the ancient theologians and not from the pre-Socratic physiologists and cosmologists, but throughout he gives them, with sovereign poetic liberty, a sublimized philosophical meaning.

Plato returns to the problem of the soul again and again in his dialogues. In the Phaedo, the Phaedrus, the Laws we find proofs of the immortality of the soul, whereas in the Timacus, Plato's great cosmogonic myth, we take a new look at the problem because the philosopher there dwells at length on the creation of the soul in his mythical story of the ψυχογονία. This part distinguishes Plato's cosmogony more than anything else from the cosmogonies of earlier Greek thinkers: when he late in life writes his own story of the origin of the universe, the most important point of difference

from his predecessors is exactly this, that the existence
of souls in it has become the central problem; and since
the soul is for Plato the principle of all motion and is
prior to the body, Plato's whole cosmogony is con-
structed around the idea of a world-soul. If Plato uses
motives of ancient Greek theology throughout, it is
obvious that they offer him the material for a completely new theology, which we see take shape in his
later works; but it is characteristic that in his outline
of a theology in the Timaeus and the Laws the soul
stands out as the basic fact. Two are the sources for
the belief in God, he writes in book XII of his Laws:
the eternal ordered movement of the stars and the
spontaneous and inexhaustible, ever-flowing life of the
soul.

We have traced Plato's philosophy of the soul
through its various phases and found it to be the principle of all life and movement in the universe. The
short time at our disposal does not permit us to discuss
in detail the various so-called proofs of the immortality
of the soul given in the Phaedo, the Republic, and the
Phaedrus, nor do I think that it would be profitable to
do so without taking into account the full context of
Plato's philosophy of being and knowledge. If in these
proofs Plato seems to make the issue depend on logical
subtleties, the great soul myths speak an unmistakable
language; for they show clearly that Plato is aware of
his trespassing the limits of rational thought and that
he feels that the mythopoeic presentation of the issue
is the only appropriate approach. Like a philosophical
Michelangelo, he puts before the eyes of humanity in
symbolic frescoes of unspeakable grandeur the divine
origin of the soul, its journey to this world of the
senses, its longing for the other world of true being, and

its return from exile to its home after due purification by philosophy. The Hebrew Bible does not know immortality in this sense at all, and the idea of resurrection in the New Testament is quite different. If nevertheless Plato's ideas of the soul and its destiny seem so familiar to us and have kept their direct appeal, that is because they have been adopted, with inevitable modifications, by the Fathers of the Church. If they dogmatized this part of Plato's philosophy of the soul, whereas in Plato himself everything remains *in suspenso*, they have this in common with the Neoplatonists, who brought it all into the form of a theological system. The Christian Fathers rejected the story of the transmigration of the soul, but they accepted the immortality of the individual soul, since they found it reconcilable with Paul's notion of the resurrection and with Jewish-Christian angelology, i.e., the existence of a world of immaterial beings. The most important fact in the history of Christian doctrine was that the father of Christian theology, Origen, was a Platonic philosopher at the school of Alexandria. He built into Christian doctrine the whole cosmic drama of the soul, which he took from Plato, and although later Christian Fathers decided that he took over too much, that which they kept was still the essence of Plato's philosophy of the soul. It was for them as it was for Plato the significant expression of their basic spiritualism and immaterialism. Socrates' message to the world presupposes a radical transvaluation of reality—so Callicles, the strong man in Plato's Gorgias, tells Socrates—and he is right. It meant the greatest revolution in human thought that had ever occurred, and the man who lived this faith and died for it had both his feet on the ground, though in a world other than that of his fellow Athenians. Standing firmly on this ground, he was strong enough to counterbalance the weight of the entire visible world and normal life. Socrates is invulnerable by the imperfection of human justice, by the majority vote of common sense, and by the logic of both scientific and unscientific materialism. The human mind cannot reach the dimension to which the soul of man belongs by way of ordinary logic. Even though Plato makes repeated attempts to rationalize his faith, it is "in the form of myth" that he gives humanity the lasting symbol of his experience of ultimate reality. He became the creator of the new myth after the primitive myth of a bygone age had had its last great revival in Greek tragedy. The point around which Plato's new myth crystallized is the soul. At the very moment when the Greek mind seemed to arrive at the stage of its final *Entmythologisierung*, a super-myth arose and ushered in a new age of the world. It was in this atmosphere that the religion of Christianity was able to establish itself and so find the new justification for the great paradox of its own supramundane faith. It could happen only in a world that spoke Greek, as has often been said; but it did not depend on the language in the linguistic sense of the κοινή. It was possible in a world that spoke the spiritual language of Plato.

As we said in the first part of this lecture, the immortality of man consisted in his name and in the living memory of his deeds, as long as the individual was safe and protected as a part of the social community of his fellow citizens in the early Greek *polis*, even after his death. The belief in another kind of immortality, rooted in the very essence of his soul, sprang from a new age that was no longer so sure of man's self-fulfillment as a part of whatever state on earth. The order of being on which Plato's philosophical man depends is to be found in the *polis* of his own soul, and with the faith in the eternal and unshakable character of this invisible being the belief in the lasting nature of the soul itself emerged triumphantly from the ruins of the political cosmos of the early and classical Hellenic world. The scholastic problems that seemed to be implied in this assertion were promptly pointed out by later ancient thinkers, who mistook the reality of the soul as either true or as unreal in the sense of the facts of natural science. Kant called immortality and God "postulates" of human reason. Plato called them "the truly being," thereby devaluating the reality of our sense perception and granting a higher reality to man's essence as a moral and spiritual being.

INTIMATIONS OF IMMORTALITY IN THE THOUGHT OF JESUS

THE INGERSOLL LECTURE FOR 1959

Henry J. Cadbury

THE historic Ingersoll lectureship on the Immortality of Man requires of the lecturer both some legitimate extension of its terms and some necessary limitation of his field. One is justified in supposing that the pious layman who planned the foundation was not thinking in highly technical terms, but like laymen of our day was thinking of a widely shared belief in the *post mortem* survival or revival of those who die. If he had wished to specify the indiscriminate persistence of the individual as a philosophical tenet of the nature of man, he could well have used the more familiar term— the immortality of the soul. On the other hand, if he had wished to be faithful to the wording of much of the Bible and to the Church's creeds, he would have spoken of the resurrection of the dead.

Earlier lecturers have taken the liberty of dealing with the nearest analogue to one or other of these concepts in a great variety of cultural situations. It has seemed to me not more out of bounds to inquire into what little evidence we have of the thought of Jesus in this area. The word immortality was perhaps not even known to him. It is scarcely an Aramaic concept. Even the whole Greek New Testament has the classical

term but two or three times. What Jesus did apparently
think of man's future, where his views are likely to have
come from, and particularly in what kind of context
they seemed to him significant are questions that are
worthy of the brief mention that the present occasion
permits.

Without overshadowing this limited subject I find
it necessary or at least desirable to deal in advance and
at some length with some modern and even some early
Christian perspectives that are unlikely to have been
shared by Jesus himself in order that we may be in a
position to conjecture and to contrast his own way of
thinking. To do so one must speak in somewhat general
terms of the New Testament as a whole, a much more
unhomogeneous body of thought, and of some problems of its interpretation. The disproportion of such
prefatory matters may be remedied by the brevity with
which the central subject can be presented.

A year ago in the Cambridge subway I was struck
by an advertisement: "You don't need eyes to see
God." I soon concluded it was not merely another text
of religious propaganda, but a solicitation for medical
purposes. I recalled that a friend of mine who had died
lately in a Boston hospital had donated her eyes for
transplanting to the living blind, and closer inspection
of the small print of the notice confirmed my conjecture with the words "Write or telephone to the Boston
Eye Bank."

What interested me was the religious implication of
the notice. It had been used, I learned, with the con-
sent of the local churches, including especially the
Roman Catholic. It was also used presumably with the
assumption that it would have meaning to the traveling

public, beyond mere church affiliation. Since the latest Gallup Poll to which I have access reported that 96 per cent of the people of America believe in God and 76 per cent believe in a life after death, the general acceptability of the slogan could be taken for granted.

Yet I can hardly believe it represents a clear or uniform view on the part of those who accept the slogan or who increasingly answer Dr. Gallup's questions in the affirmative. The biblical teaching is not clear whether either here or hereafter anyone sees God with these eyes. They are rather a figure of speech for what American theologians were calling a few years ago *New Eyes for Invisibles* or *Eyes of Faith*.[1] It should be easy for us therefore to imagine a similar undefinedness in the first-century Church among those who at that time took for granted both the belief in God and the belief in life after death.

The New Testament root of the latter was primarily the Jewish resurrection belief. This was based on the eschatological view of history such as is found in the books we call apocalypses. It is doubtful whether it occurs in the older books like Job and the Psalms,[2] though passages from both have been taken in the later sense, much as in the New Testament certain passages which do imply resurrection have had read into them the quite different doctrine of immortality. One Old Testament book, Koheleth, or Ecclesiastes, seems definitely to deny after life—in spite of the glorious, though perhaps mistranslated, text, "He hath set eternity in their heart" (3:11).

[1] Titles of books by Rufus M. Jones, 1943, and Paul S. Minear, 1946, respectively.

[2] Cf. most recently C. S. Lewis, *Reflections on the Psalms* (1958), Chapter 5.

If historical and critical studies are to be trusted, it was first in the Maccabean period that a special situation gave rise to a resurrection belief. There was a new hope of a better day near at hand. It was precipitated by persecution as hope often is, but the persecution raised a special problem. The martyrs who had been most loyal of all were likely to miss the consummation while the lukewarm or the lucky survivors might share it. The book of Daniel by a leap of faith, trusting in God's justice, declares: "Many of those that sleep in the dust of the earth shall awake, some to everlasting life, and some to shame and everlasting contempt" (12:2).

There is a curious parallel in what is perhaps our oldest extant Christian document, I Thessalonians. Again the hope of a near denouement burned with special brightness. Its imminence was calculated (as in Daniel), perhaps overcalculated. In the expectant group at Thessalonica some already had died. In addition to other reasons for sorrow their surviving friends saw no justice in their being cheated of the common Christian reward. So Paul consoles them with assurance:

> But we would not have you ignorant, brethren, concerning those who are asleep, that you may not grieve as others do who have no hope. For since we believe that Jesus died and rose again, even so, through Jesus, God will bring with him those who have fallen asleep. For this we declare to you by the word of the Lord, that we who are alive, who are left until the coming of the Lord, shall not precede those who have fallen asleep. For the Lord himself will descend from heaven with a cry of command, with the archangel's call, and with the sound of the trumpet of God. And the dead in Christ will rise first; then we who are alive, who are

left, shall be caught up together with them in the clouds to meet the Lord in the air; and so we shall always be with the Lord. Therefore comfort one another with these words (I Thess. 4:13–18 RSV).

As Paul says elsewhere (I Cor. 15:17, 18), without such a promise one must conclude that those who have fallen asleep in Christ, i.e., deceased Christians, have perished.

Thus in both Old Testament and New Testament the resurrection belief enters as an exception, as a problem of a minority. But with the apocalyptic hope deferred the minority who have died or will die becomes a majority. What was exceptional was universalized, at least by one influential sect, the Pharisees, and by Christians including perhaps in time Paul himself.

Another factor in the New Testament is the belief in the resurrection of Jesus. The relation of this to the wider belief is ambiguous. In fact the term resurrection is today often used confusedly, meaning now the individual instance of Jesus, now the anticipation of a wider occurrence. One is a past event, one is future. The past event is treated as a foretaste, or firstfruits, of the future. Paul uses it as assurance of the future— briefly in I Thessalonians, more at length in I Corinthians. Whether he regarded it as occurring in the same form as the future one—and it is this which he principally is discussing in I Cor. 15—one cannot tell. If he did, the accounts in the gospels hardly agree with him. In fact, their view of the same body, scars and all, flesh and bones (Luke 24:39; John 20:25, 27; contrast "flesh and blood cannot inherit," etc. I Cor. 15:50) is antithetical to what Paul says of the more general resurrection. The Corinthians who caviled at Paul's teaching as incredible would find little satisfaction in the resurrection stories in the Gospels if they met them currently in circulation or read them later.

The experiences that led early Christians to believe Jesus was risen are obscure. They may have been partly related to the future expectation current in apocalyptic circles. If he was soon to take part as they expected in a final role it was natural to think he would rise ultimately, or indeed had risen and was in the interim *Messias absconditus*. More decisive for such a belief would be any kind of vivid sense that Jesus was still or again in contact with them—visible in heaven (Stephen in Acts), or on earth, or audible in dreams or visions (Paul in Acts). Even these are only causes for inferences to be made that he had risen. Whether the stories of the empty grave are inferences from these or whether the beliefs in his resurrection are inferences from the empty grave is uncertain. All these beliefs could arise in any order and would tend in the end to confirm one another.

Behind any or all of these is doubtless the current Jewish belief in resurrection of some people—not any belief in immortality, nor indeed a general resurrection nor what we should call today parapsychology or spiritualism. Whatever experience or convictions the first Christians had in connection with the Jesus who had been crucified would be conditioned by the current abstract resurrection belief if it were at all possible, and would be interpreted in its terms.

Conversely this single episode when so interpreted would immensely strengthen that same resurrection belief. It seemed to Paul in I Cor. 15 and elsewhere, and to his biographer in Acts, the strongest assurance. For others than Jesus, resurrection was in the future, hence uncertain. With Jesus it was in the past, and "only the past is secure." But, along with the Holy Spirit, it was a guarantee of the future. Both of them are called "firstfruits." The resurrection of Jesus sets the pattern for other cases. "As in Adam all die, so in Christ shall all be made alive." What Jesus and Paul and their contemporaries had come to accept in the abstract, now after Easter because of this single concrete instance, became more credible and more assured. Unlike the Jews, the Christians now could argue with more assurance for the extension of one certified phenomenon. What God had done, God could do. This was a method of argument that non-Christian Jews and pagans could not withstand. Their only defense was to doubt or deny the resurrection of Jesus. Probably on this rather than on the general belief the controversy turned.

If what has been said in the preceding paragraphs is correct, we get something very much like arguing in a circle. If the *post mortem* experience of Jesus was interpreted in terms of the Jewish belief in the resurrection of the just, then the Christian belief in the latter rested in turn at least in part upon the former as so interpreted. Such a circular process ought not to disturb us or surprise us. Our trouble is that when we look at a group of long-established beliefs we tend to forget their genetic character. Though we cannot always at this late date determine the sequence of their origin we should be prepared to believe that they once were either inferences from or presuppositions of one another. Their logical consistency is due precisely to this human process rather than to a more objective foundation. In such circumstances it becomes quite easy to argue in a circle, if that is the right way to describe the matter.

The effect of the belief in Jesus' resurrection on the early Christian belief in the wider resurrection experience can hardly be overestimated. It was the kind of assurance, contemporary and concrete, that the most ardent though speculative convictions of Pharisees or other non-Christian Jews could not have equaled. And it has played a major role in the continuing Christian hope.

But before leaving this factor in the subject one should remember how complicated were the forces at work in connection with the early Easter story. Even without the uncongenial or irreconcilable spiritualizing presentation by Paul, the gospel narratives themselves suggest contradiction or combination of more than one point of view or motive. The apologetic element is obvious, though, like much apologetic of all kinds, it tends to be inconsistent or even contradictory. The details given look sometimes like afterthoughts more than like the original sources of the convictions. This does nothing to reduce our certainty that Jesus' resurrection was firmly believed in, nor does it necessarily affect our historical judgment about what actually did or did not happen. There was no clear pattern in the underlying Jewish anticipation that would force the Christian story of Jesus' resurrection into a ready-made mold.

There were in fact other aspects of Judaism which both before and after the events of Easter the first Christians shared.

(1) One of these was quite different from any resurrection belief—the belief that in individual instances men had escaped death altogether. They were quite literally immortal—not in the sense that having died once they would live forever, but in the sense that they

had not died and perhaps would not die. Instead of death and descent into Sheol they had experienced removal—ascension, assumption, rapture, are the names theology has used—and the instances first noted by the Jews and Christians, though differently described, are Enoch, Elijah, and probably Moses. Elements of such belief are closely associated with Christian views of the resurrection, whether that of Jesus or that of Christians in general. In both of these, real death was taken for granted. Indeed orthodox Christianity was concerned to stress—perhaps against docetism—that Jesus really died (Ignatius), and was buried (Paul, the Creeds), instead of being removed at once from the cross (Gospel of Peter) or before the cross to God and heaven. Instead of such prompt assumption, opportunity for appearances of the risen Jesus was required in a period of sojourn on earth whether forty days (Acts) or some briefer or much longer period. The ascension belief was not fully rejected. It was added to resurrection belief. It is implied not only in the explicit narrative in Acts 1, but in other passages of Luke-Acts, in John and Paul. There is no clear distinction between appearances of the risen Jesus that assume he has already been thus exalted and those which at least by context defer such exaltation.

(2) Another aspect of pre-Christian belief which fits very neatly here and which also had, I believe, much to do with the Christian belief in the resurrection of Jesus is the expectation of the coming of the Messiah. In the nature of the case this expectation had no fixed features in Judaism, and various forms of it are reflected in the Gospels. Certainly some people held that when he came it would be after prior existence and not completely *de novo* and others that the place from which

he came was not a matter of general knowledge. Now early after Jesus' death and perhaps before, he was identified with this coming Messiah, and it was therefore natural that his availability for this future role should be indicated. Of course availability did not require an immediate resurrection. Fourth Ezra, a Jewish writing probably of the first Christian century, speaks of the Messiah as remaining dead for a long period. But the Christian church while it looked for the *parousia* in the rather imminent future found in the view that the Messiah had been promptly raised (Does "the third day" of I Cor. 15:4 and elsewhere not emphasize this promptness?) an assurance of this eschatological hope. Jesus was immediately available in the sense that he was not in Sheol or in the grave, but was in heaven or at God's right hand, whence in any case the events of the last day were likely to be initiated. Thus the eschatological hope of Judaism was a conditioning factor not only for the pre-Christian and Christian belief in the plural resurrection "at the last day" but also for the particular Christian belief in the individual and exceptional prior resurrection of Jesus.

Perhaps the dependence of these Christian beliefs on the primitive Jewish-Christian eschatology is not generally realized by modern believers. This is, however, a minor embarrassment compared with the fact that the very notion of messiahship is dependent on the same circle of ideas, and with it the core for any superlative view of the person and work of Jesus Christ. Insofar as the primitive eschatology is outgrown or abandoned as myth, we must admit that modern beliefs in the significance of Jesus of Nazareth and also beliefs in his or our afterlife are by-products or survivals or developments of the archaic and outmoded dreams of the apocalyptic dreamers. There is nothing unusual in the persistence of partial elements of myth when the myth as a whole is discredited. If they persist by sheer inertia that is natural. But the thoughtful or conscientious Christian today will welcome the discovery of this ancestry in order that he may inquire further into the motives of their origin and the relevance of those motives for today.

Before we attempt to do so, something should be said about the word myth. It is somewhat ambiguous and is perhaps unnecessarily offensive. It is used of stories of the past, connected with religion, and aiming to explain the origin of beliefs or practices. This is not the sense in which I have employed it. It is also used of the future, of dreams or prophecies of what from the time of the mythmaker is yet to take place. In the nature of things the imaginative factor is in such predictions peculiarly strong. Actually they rarely use much of the available data for conjecturing what will probably happen. They are even more fallible than political forecasts based on public opinion polls or than weather predictions made by scientific meteorologists. If they have validity it must be credited to the supernatural foresight of inspired prophets and seers. Natural calculation or astute insight would rarely be an acceptable explanation to religious believers in these myths.

There is a third sense in which today theologians seem to use the word or the root, though not of the narrative content of an idea so much as of its framework. It means the *Weltanschauung* in which people express themselves, whether about things past, things contemporary, or things future. Demythicizing (demythologizing) is the attempt to strip away from religious thought such elements as belong to transient and unscientific cosmology or psychology. In the former belongs the three-story universe, the earth with heaven above and hell beneath, in the second belong the mythical beings like demons and angels.

If this process is justified as applied to narratives in the Gospels of the New Testament which appear to have a kernel of history, we can hardly object if it is applied to the purely futuristic ideas of life after death. That the dead become angels and exist in heaven would be the kind of mythical views that would be the first to disappear at the hands of modern demythologizing. Probably we are quite prepared to surrender heaven as a place literally in the sky, and the angels as corporeal beings with or without wings. The purpose of demythologizing is to remove the shell of such notions in order that the spiritual values can be preserved and translated into terms congenial to our own *Weltanschauung,* and existential, that is, relevant to our need.

One cannot, however, resist the temptation to ask why do we stop the process of removal just where these scholars do. If some of the furnishings of religious setting in the past happen to be more congenial to the present, are they thereby the more real? Are not myth and symbol almost universal in religion? almost inevitable? The presence of the naïve and archaic in parts of the New Testament language ought rather to warn us of the same element of myth in the rest, even though we find it easier to accept.

"Poetry," writes a modern literary critic, "is the imaginative dominion over experience." The same can be said for religion. Religion tends to personalize and materialize its contents. It operates through dramatization. Besides angels and demons it has other characters, *dramatis personae*, God, Jesus, Satan, with whom men have to do. Their relationship to us is conceived much as of actors on a stage. The myth of *Heilsgeschichte* is an imaginative narration of describable transactions. It can be as definite as the plot of a novel, and fiction in turn can be as objective and realistic as the prose facts of history.

There are children who are particularly addicted to fantasy. With or without the use of dolls they live at times in a make-believe world of fictitious characters living in human fashion, with all the characteristic features of events in experience. Perhaps this persistence of imagination is one of the charming features of childhood that Wordsworth had in mind in his famous ode. And imagination naturally plays its part in thinking of life after death. But we must recognize precisely that it is imagination and that its figures are taken—whether mystical or existentialist—from other scenes. As it was in the days of Noah, so shall it be in the days of the Son of Man, and so it is in childhood's fantasy: they eat, they drink, they buy and sell, they marry or are given in marriage. I am not concerned now to challenge the legitimacy and value of all such symbolic aspects of religion. It is only fair to ask that they be recognized, and recognized within the cautious line of what is called reality as well as beyond it.

It has already been mentioned that demythologizing is somewhat destructive of certain categories of space, the ancient Semitic view of a universe in layers. But another ancient category and one not obsolete is the category of time. Our Jewish-Christian tradition is especially given to this. One need merely be reminded of the use of age, or ages. Time extends from the age to the ages of the ages. Life for men is in this age and then in the age to come. History may be described in the book of reigns (as the Greek entitles our Book of Kings). The supreme ideal is described in a time word—the reign of God. It is perhaps characteristic of the difference between the Hellenic and Semitic, that when they symbolize value concretely the former tends to do so geographically, the latter chronologically.

In Christianity, both ancient and modern, the category of time has played a large part. Religion is understood as revealed in history. God deals with men in successive dispensations, and is known by his actions in time. The past set of covenants which form the framework of the Pentateuch shares this outlook as does the simpler division of history that one finds in Paul. In the first the events are the Sabbath (Creation), kosher food (Noah), circumcision (Abraham), the final law (Moses). For Paul the intervals are "from Adam to Moses," from Moses to Christ, and until Christ's return.

In modern Christianity the same temporal representations are favorite. The concept of evolution has made them attractive to liberal and secular thinkers. There is little criticism of the linear concept of the Old Testament or New as applied to time to match the demythologizing of the spatial concepts of vertically separated levels. In general "Biblical theology" seems to have given the time element a new lease of life. Cullmann's title *Christ and Time*[3] is topical, and so are the overtones of phrases like *Heilsgeschichte* and "Christ event." Von Hügel described the Fourth Gospel quite differently. He says of it, "There is everywhere a striving

[3] See James Muilenburg, "The Biblical View of Time," *Harvard Theological Review* 54 (1961), 225–252; cf. James Barr, *Biblical Words for Time* (1962).

to contemplate history *sub specie aeternitatis* and to englobe the successiveness of men in the simultaneity of God."[4] But John seems not to have many followers. The successiveness of men is not objected to. *Post mortem* existence does not conflict with standards of myth widely acceptable today and not requiring substitution. Any discussion of immortality must emphasize that in every form it is a conception subject to the common human category of sense of time.

This unquestioned acceptability in many quarters is all the more striking since pre-existence—projecting from man's visible existence in the other direction—is one of the things that some of our demythologizing friends have ruled out. For the same reason they must be willing to exclude a *post mortem* existence both for Jesus and at the last day for those who believe in him. If they find currently unacceptable the view held by more than one New Testament writer that before Jesus' birth or incarnation he had enjoyed a noteworthy existence comparable to his later exaltation, the latter must be rejected also. The two belong together. Interestingly enough, Wordsworth accepted as an intimation of future immortality precisely what he called "intimations" of prenatal existence.

Actually contemporary theologians—and I name no names—are not agreed as to where the demythologizing should begin and end. The imaginative spheres to which the expression of religious experience are transposed include several—chronology, theology and anthropology, as well as cosmology. Which of these categories may we retain in the primitive New Testament form, and which must be demythologized? Uncon-

[4] *Encyclopaedia Britannica*, s.v. John, Gospel of St.

sciously we tend to retain part and revise part. Each person wishes to salvage what seems meaningful to himself. To others the full biblical *Weltanschauung* appears to be a kind of seamless robe to be either accepted or rejected in its entirety.

The need for demythologizing the futuristic hope of the first Christians was evidently felt, if not expressed, in an early period of Christian history. For ultimately and in some respects quite soon much of it was translated to other forms of expression; if one may use the word, it was remythologized. Something like the Greek Platonic view of immortality unconsciously modified the expression of normative Jewish resurrection beliefs. We suspect this already in Paul, as we are reasonably sure of it in Josephus' description of Pharisaism. But as often happens, the old and new continued side by side in uneasy juxtaposition, and without the thorough supremacy of either view. The gradual increase of the immortality concept can no doubt be traced, and its reasons understood. The parallel persistence of the doctrine of bodily resurrection, not merely because of the authority of the New Testament and the Creeds but also because of human nature's craving for the familiar assurance of sensory phenomena, is also intelligible.

There are both advantages and disadvantages in focusing our inquiry upon the teachings of Jesus. The advantages are these: Whatever he thought or felt about the future during his ministry is little likely to have been influenced by his own later resurrection. For his followers, as we have already noted, this event, accepted as a past fact of experience, had a great influence when they looked backward or when they looked forward to the more general resurrection in the future. Our Synoptic Gospels record sayings of Jesus anticipating that he would not only be killed, but also would "rise after three days."[5] But the genuineness of the sayings may be doubted, or in any case the effect of the actual event is not likely to have acted in advance on the mind of Jesus or the minds of those who heard him. Only afterwards did the individual event that was past play a part in visualizing and confirming the collective event that was future, as indeed it affected nearly every phase of Christian thinking.

Before his death Jesus and his disciples were spared the problem that has bothered men ever since, even down to the recent publication of a teacher in this school,[6] the relation of a resurrection conceived as an historical event to future theological belief. Epistemology seems to ask more difficult questions about actual events than about merely anticipated events.

Furthermore, Jesus unlike us moderns, though not unlike his early followers, found little difficulty with the miracle involved in resurrection from the dead. That it was or would be supernatural rather than natural, if one may use a distinction scarcely known to him, he very likely took for granted. Several stories of individuals raised from the dead by Jesus or Peter or Paul are reported by the Synoptic writers much as are the stories of miraculous cure of the sick. For the whole of the New Testament we may be sure that the all-penetrating theism of the outlook on nature and his-

[5] Mark 8:31; 9:31; 10:34. The parallels say "on the third day," and, in Matthew, "be raised." In general resurrection is expressed in the New Testament as "from the dead" ($\dot{\epsilon}\kappa \ \nu\epsilon\kappa\rho\hat{\omega}\nu$) not "of the dead."

[6] R. R. Niebuhr, *Resurrection and Historical Reason* (1957).

tory left unraised the question whether resurrection from the dead was an automatic process inherent in the constitution of man, as in some other cultures the continuance of immortal souls is felt to be. On the contrary it was believed that only God could give power to raise the dead, and Jesus and his contemporaries, even in their more critical moods, were little concerned to question the possibility of what God had done and would do.

Finally Jesus' views of afterlife are unlikely to have been affected by what we call the Greek conception. Some Jews of that general period, through contact with things unsemitic, may have been influenced by the doctrine of immortality. It is more likely to be found in the Apocrypha of the Old Testament and in Jewish apocalypses than in the Hebrew or rabbinic writings. I think Greek influence on Ecclesiastes has not been made out.

What concerns us here is the probability that Jesus himself was less likely to conflate with Jewish conceptions of resurrection alien parallels than were Paul, the authors of Hebrews and of John, and even than the authors of Luke-Acts and of the other Synoptic Gospels. How alien, not to say mutually exclusive, the two concepts are to each other was brought to our attention by Professor Cullmann in his recent Ingersoll Lecture. And it is well to remind ourselves of the clear-cut words of Justin Martyr in his Dialogue with Trypho, written after a full century of Christianity:

> If you have met with some so-called Christians who do not accept this [resurrection and millenium] but dare to blaspheme the God of Abraham, the God of Isaac and the God of Jacob who affirm that there is

no resurrection of the dead but that when they die their souls are taken up to heaven, do not suppose that they are Christians. . . . But I and any Christians who are orthodox on all points know that there will be a resurrection of the flesh, etc. (ch. 80).

The disadvantages of focusing our attention upon Jesus' view of the afterlife are also obvious. His thought must if possible be discovered behind the reported sayings in the Gospels, especially the first three of them. This is a familiar difficulty whenever one seeks to get at his mind on any subject. But it is not only the ultimate evangelist that has to be allowed for. Between him and Jesus, oral if not written tradition has been at work altering and varying the original viewpoint. This accounts for most of the apparent discrepancies among the Synoptic sayings of Jesus, since the single units of tradition had passed through different media in the process. Even the original expressions of Jesus might well have seemed to us obscure or contradictory as do those of Paul from whom we have firsthand records in his genuine letters. In the case of Jesus unresolved variations of viewpoint about the afterlife are fully as apparent.

Beside all this we shall find the amount of relevant material rather scanty. No matter how abundant Jesus' references to the future appear to be—and none of the devices of scholarship has yet succeeded in reducing the extent to which we have come to recognize the futuristic element in the teaching of Jesus—on certain aspects of that future, Jesus has in our records less to say than might have been expected. The resurrection as distinct from the judgment is not often separately described, nor is the nature of life after the judgment.

As in many other Christian sources much less is said of the fate of the condemned than of the blessed, and much less about individuals than about groups.

This paucity of clear exposition is intelligible if we are right in thinking that whatever our temporary focus now may be it was not a major concern of Jesus to expound or reassert the views of the future life which he held or shared. His references to it are mainly incidental, and associated in a subordinate way with his major interests. This is increasingly clear of the whole complex of ideas which we call eschatology to which our present subject belongs. Even the Kingdom of God for all its frequency of mention in our records is not the central concern of the Gospels. The same may be said of the resurrection or "eternal life." Their mention is nearly always incidental to something else.

Perhaps this is most readily illustrated in the Beatitudes, where we have in each sentence first a selected quality or condition for which men are to be congratulated and then in the second line of each couplet a variety of expressions of reward—"Theirs is the Kingdom of Heaven" (twice), "They shall see God," "They shall be called sons of God," "Your reward is great in heaven." Not all the references are *post mortem*, though some plainly are, and others are ambiguous or indecisive in their implications of time. Insofar as they are *post mortem* they refer to reward or punishment, to advantage or disadvantage, to gain or loss. They are parallel to incidental references of more immediate results to the living.

On the resurrection itself Jesus once is represented as being drawn out in debate. The passage occurs in Mark and is reproduced in Matthew and Luke in evident dependence upon Mark (Mark 12:18–27; Matt.

22:23–33; Luke 20:27–38). The passage belongs to the category and to the series of test questions. Sadducees, who as a group deny the resurrection, are the questioners and frame a question intended to reduce the idea to absurdity by instancing one woman who by Levirate law for childless widows had been married in turn to seven brothers. The question is asked, Whose wife will she be in the resurrection? (Incidentally this is perhaps the first place in the Bible where monogamy is most definitely assumed.)

Jesus' reply plainly accepts and argues for the doctrine of the resurrection. It disposes of the supposed assumption of plural marriage by declaring that when they rise from the dead they neither marry nor ar given in marriage but are like angels in heaven. (Again it may seem odd that the clearest descriptive datum of the future life in the Gospels is the absence of marriage— a view which some of the rabbis shared though others denied.) In the reply Jesus also meets not the specific instance but the skepticism about the resurrection belief by declaring that his questioners are wrong because they "know neither the scriptures nor the power of God." These are both of them points made by the rabbis in debate. God's power to raise the dead, they claim, is no greater than his power to create men by birth—an *a fortiori* argument that must be accepted. This is not explicitly included in the Gospel passage. But it does include a typical argument from scripture:

> But as for the dead being raised, have you not read in the book of Moses, in the passage about the Bush, how God said to him "I am the God of Abraham, the God of Isaac, the God of Jacob"? He is not God of the dead but of the living. You are quite wrong.

The argument here is characteristically Jewish.[7] The rabbis, and I think other Jews and Christians, deduced contemporaneity of Moses with the patriarchs from pronouns and tenses and other grammatical phenomena in the texts of scripture. What God said to Moses involves survival or revival for Abraham, Isaac and Jacob. It is because they anticipated this future that, according to Heb. 11:16, "God is not ashamed to be called their God." Similarly according to John 8:56, Abraham had seen the day of Christ.

This single synoptic passage is in its general tenor self-evidently Jewish. It clearly puts Jesus on the side of the belief in resurrection along with the Pharisees, the rabbis, and presumably the weight of official Judaism going back as far as the second benediction in the daily prayer of Eighteen (Shemoneh Esreh). I see no reason why this Jewishness, or this concern for a theological question unusual in these Gospels (but compare the discussion of the Messiah's sonship in the very next section) should lead us to doubt the correctness of its ascription to Jesus of an acceptance of current ideas. At least he was no Sadducee. Luke who makes some changes in the words of Jesus here does not pass beyond the range of current Jewish speculation.

The other and minor references to the subject of future life do not match this one synoptic passage in directness or explicitness. They are, as has been said, incidental. Only once again is any general resurrection mentioned, though it is described as the resurrection of the righteous. In Luke 14:14, in a passage comparing the result of dinner invitations extended respectively

---

[7] See my *The Peril of Modernizing Jesus* (1937, reprinted 1962), pp. 59f., 61–63, with notes.

to one's associates or equals and to the underprivileged, Jesus explains that the first will return the invitation while the others cannot, but "you will be repaid at the resurrection of the just." The reference here to the righteous only cannot be pressed since the same evangelist elsewhere writes that "there will be a resurrection of both the righteous and the unrighteous" (Acts 24:15).

There is also in Luke (16:19–31) the parable of the rich man and Lazarus where, as in some of the Beatitudes, and especially in the woes and beatitudes of Luke, compensation is conspicuous rather by ways of reversal or equalization than as reward and punishment. As Abraham said to the rich man, "Son, remember that you in your lifetime received your good things and Lazarus in like manner evil things; but now he is comforted here and you are in anguish."

This parable is noteworthy in other respects; the situation is pictured prior to any resurrection. Both of the deceased have been transported promptly to Hades, where they occupy two compartments separated by "a great gulf" but not preventing intercommunication. One is pleasant, the bosom of Abraham, the other a place of torment with the anguish of flame.

It is worthwhile to pause here to remind ourselves how often Abraham or all three of the patriarchs represent in Christian documents the charter members, or the hosts, or the primary examples of the resurrection experience. Beside this reference to Abraham as presiding over the situation between Dives and Lazarus, we have already mentioned the answer of Jesus to the Sadducees in Mark 12 and parallels and the passages in John 8 and in Heb. 11 and from a later period the statement of Justin Martyr that to deny the resurrection is to blaspheme the God of Abraham, the God of Isaac and the God of Jacob. There is also the earlier saying in Matt. 8:11 (cf. Luke 13:28, from Q ?) which anticipates the same three as the nucleus of membership in the Kingdom of God: "I tell you many will come from east and west and will recline at table with Abraham, Isaac, and Jacob in the kingdom of heaven." Perhaps the same reason underlies the mention of the same three in Acts 3:13 in a context referring ("glorified"; "raised from the dead") to the resurrection of Jesus. Assurance in the resurrection of the patriarchs, though differently arrived at from the assurance in the resurrection of Jesus, seems to have served in Judaism and Jewish Christianity the same purpose as "firstfruits" which that of Jesus did later.

The concept of reward or punishment undeferred at death recurs also in another Lucan passage where Jesus on the cross says to the penitent thief, "Today you will be with me in paradise" (Luke 23:43).

This is not the place for the collection and minute examination of all synoptic passages relevant to our topic. That has been done by others and it leaves a confused and contradictory impression. Not even when the words of Jesus are compared with the more abundant Jewish materials and are found to coincide with them, whether from the apocalypses, from the Hellenistic writings, or from Talmud and Midrash, is the situation much better. Evidently the several sources exercised much freedom in imagining the subject, in recasting and varying the imagery. Even matters of place and time, or places and times, in the *post mortem* experience of the dead were not consistently plotted and mapped. The reasons can be easily guessed—the inherent unreality of the subject, the consequent conjecture and inference based on the equally fragmentary and unprecise statements in scripture, and the fusion of ideals of collective or national destiny with the problems of individual fate. There is inevitable vacillation between what is conceived as happening to the individual at once after death, and what occurs simultaneously to all men at the time of the final judgment. Approximate differentiation of good and evil men seems desirable both at once and ultimately. Hence one gets in other sources such implications or combinations as a first and a second death, a first and second resurrection, the days of the Messiah and the Kingdom of God. Whether the scene of these events is the earth as we know it or as it will be transformed, or elsewhere—Hades, Gehenna, heaven, paradise or "the eternal habitations" (Luke 16:9)—is equally ambiguous.

Even if we had more words of Jesus on the subject and if we were sure they were all correctly reported one may doubt whether they would add up to a blueprint that would carry even for the devout believer a satisfying and authoritative picture as of a principal concern of Jesus' teaching. The very incidental character of the references suggests alike two almost contradictory conclusions.

1. The afterlife was taken for granted by Jesus and by his hearers generally. He did not need to impress it or correct it. It was not for him or them a question of hesitation and debate. It is therefore an assured ingredient of his perspective.

2. By the same token his allusions do not allow us to reconstruct any very definite or circumstantial impression of this future. They were innocently unprecise, intimations rather than descriptions, and were em-

ployed in connection with other matters on which Jesus had something emphatic and significant to say.

In other words, the more sure we are that Jesus in fact accepted the perspective of those who believe in future existence, the more evident it seems that it was not the center of his interest but was thought of and felt as relevant to questions of here and now. For him and for us it was part of the morrow about which neither he nor we need be anxious. If death of the body is not to be feared, if one is to go his way today and tomorrow whatever the third day has in store, there is no need for the comforting thoughts of an after-life to banish the fear of death. We have lately had from the pen of John Knox a very honest inquiry into the problem of knowing what Jesus' death meant in anticipation to Jesus himself.[8] It will be more difficult to answer a like question about his personal and private employment of any anticipation of survival or revival. Our oldest records report primarily what was extrovert about him, and I think we must confine ourselves to this aspect of our records if we are to escape the extremes of fanciful imagination.

We cannot assume that the ideas and motives that had marked the origin of the resurrection faith in late Judaism always remained emphatic nor that the meanings that later Christians have found in it were already in the thought of Jesus. Clearly certain English words into which his sayings have been translated have come to have for us connotations that were not in their originals. "Eternal" ($a\iota\omega\nu\iota o\varsigma$) lacked its emphasis upon endlessness, though not on futurity. "Heaven" lacked the modern suggestion of futurity though not

8 John Knox, *The Death of Christ* (1958), Chapter 5.

of otherworldliness. With one possible exception[9] neither "soul" nor "spirit" is used in the futuristic sense. Just as Jews and Christians have read into Old Testament passages a belief in resurrection that was not there, so more recent Christians have read into New Testament passages a belief in immortality instead of resurrection.

The religious and philosophical values of a future life to Jesus were perhaps less self-centered than they were later. There was an altruistic element in the anxiety of the living about the dead, as we understand the passages already cited from Daniel and 1 Thessalonians. The living needed assurance that the deserving dead would not miss the good things that the righteous living expected, and (in Daniel) that the wicked who had died would not escape the penalty that was their due. Resurrection, as distinct from immortality, is not the avoidance of death but revival after death. The length of interval between death and revival is not indicated. If Jesus sometimes emphasizes the nearness of the Kingdom he is shortening the interval not so much for the dead as for the many living who would "not taste of death." Obviously this differs a good deal from any modern concern for the situation *after death*.

There is no evidence that for Jesus the after life was regarded as showing that values in this life are durable and therefore precious. Nor on the other hand is it an expression of the opposite of this life with the latter's mutability. It spells neither continuity nor discontinuity, neither unity nor the kind of duality which is so

[9] Matt. 10:28. Cf. H. B. Sharman, *The Teaching of Jesus about the Future* (1909), pp. 267–270.

natural in our tendency to contrast the material and the spiritual, the secular and the sacred. Such philosophical approaches are not typical of Jesus.

Today it is a satisfying belief that the future life will have social attraction—the company of those whom we have loved and unimpeded fellowship with God. This ideal is not explicit in the limited Gospel material and probably not implicit. There is more if not better company in the wide road that leads to destruction than in the narrow one leading to life. To meet modern tastes one would have to spiritualize such descriptions as we have of dining in the Kingdom of God and to deliteralize the fire in Gehenna and gnashing of teeth in the outer darkness. If Jesus tells the penitent thief, "Today you will be with me in paradise," the accent is on the place or time, not the company.

References to the future life for Jesus as for Judaism in general are connected with the idea of retribution. It may not be clear whether that life itself is retributive to the good alone, or whether resurrection is prior to a judgment at which rewards and penalties are allotted, or mainly a subsequent period in which they are carried out. Whatever the extent or the sequence visualized concerning resurrection, judgment and ultimate *post mortem* experience, these are part of an inseparable group of ideas and have to do with the consequences of our behavior here. Formally at least the future is the sanction for what is recommended now. Insofar as that future is after death, or without death at the *parousia*, or even in the normal nearer sequels in this age—and often the sayings of Jesus put these parallel, or leave them undistinguished—the recommendations are intended to warn or promise. This utilitarian-sounding approach would suit the standpoint of his hearers. Jesus' own difference of emphasis would lie in what he recommends, not on why he recommends it. Even sacrificial, disinterested conduct is rarely mentioned by him without appeal to future consequence.

This appeal to the future may have been conventional. Jesus does not seem concerned to give instruction about the future for its own sake. Recommendations on conduct here and now were his main concern. Since he felt these to be valid, self-evident—or in religious language, the will of God—he was sure they deserved and would receive, sooner or later, due reward, and their opposites likewise the reverse. He may have emphasized the nearness of the end, the shortness of the time and the consequent urgency of right action. In so doing he was not revising the future program, or making special claims for himself, but out of "pastoral" concern was underscoring the importance of the critical choices or changes which men have to make.[10]

Such is the context in which the scattered allusions to man's fate after death occur in the older Gospels. They do not suggest a high degree of otherworldliness. They are related and relevant to behavior in this life. They leave unanswered a whole host of modern questions about the biological and psychological nature of man, about death and consciousness, about personality. They give us little for a twentieth-century prospectus on the future—even for a tidy first-century eschatology.

More offensive than what they omit is what they imply. The synoptic intimations of a future existence are in the form of sanctions for recommended conduct.

[10] The ethical implications of such sanction are well discussed by A. N. Wilder, *Eschatology and Ethics in the Teaching of Jesus* (rev. ed. 1950).

No matter how wise and true the ethical standards or the futuristic insights, their association is likely to seem a scandal. One merely cannot say which seems worse to a kind of present-day religion. Is it worse that goodness here and now should be recommended by regard for future reward and threat and that disinterested virtue should be associated with practical utilitarian considerations? Or is it worse that the spiritual ideal, which over the centuries has been refined and expressed in terms of the state of the blessed dead, should be debased by being traced back to the crude motivation in this life of escaping future punishment or gaining future rewards?

I understand that some have felt that a recent Ingersoll lecturer described the New Testament faith in the future as the wrong kind.[11] They will perhaps feel that today it is being attributed to "the wrong reason." Yet it is inevitable that this element should appear here as it does everywhere else in the Gospels. It has been described as "the perpetual twofold issue of all preaching of the gospel: the offer of mercy and the threat of impending judgment inseparable from it, deliverance and fear, salvation and destruction, life and death."[12] This, if anything, is an authentic feature of Jesus' teaching.

Can we go any further than this? Or shall we abandon Jesus' eschatology *in toto* as part of outgrown myth and start fresh from the framework of our modern thought, ethical, philosophical and scientific, to construct our own hypothesis concerning a future life?

---

[11] O. Cullmann's Ingersoll Lecture in this volume.
[12] J. Jeremias, *The Parables of Jesus* (Eng. transl., rev. ed., 1963), p. 18.

The paucity and incidental character of Jesus' references can be interpreted as justifying such treatment. It has been suggested that Jesus usually and deliberately was silent on these themes.[13] The answer to the Sadducees may show him impatient of the crudity of the view of the after life without attempting to substitute a more spiritual view. There is a specially striking conclusion—"punch line," in the vernacular— of the story of Dives and Lazarus. When the rich man wishes his surviving brothers warned of the torment of the damned by a messenger actually sent from Hades, he receives the answer, "If they do not hear Moses and the prophets neither will they be convinced if some one should rise from the dead." Twice Dives urges that such a messenger could successfully warn them so that they would repent. Twice Abraham indicates that resurrection has no convincing evidential value, when compared with scriptural warning already available. According to this word, so surprising for any early Christian document, reformed conduct in this life would not be promoted by more convincing evidence of the future life or judgment. What Jesus omits to emphasize in his teaching about the future is no great loss. It would add no useful influence.

Of course we can attempt to find behind his life and teaching presuppositions which at least for us would be logical and valid, though they too may be conventional in his environment. There is the belief in God, who has a will and that will is man's duty.

---

[13] It is noteworthy how often students of this field while admitting that Jesus shared the usual views on resurrection and general eschatology have concluded that "he felt very little interest in them." So, for example, W. G. Kümmel, *Promise and Fulfilment* (Eng. transl., 1957), p. 92. Cf. the older statements, as in B. H. Streeter, *Immortality* (1917), pp. 122f.

Those who disobey and those who obey will be treated according to their works. But beside this divine *lex talionis* there are two rather different principles at work. One is the idea that independently of individual merit God in the end equalizes good and bad experience for all men, so that evil now will be balanced with good hereafter and vice versa. This lies behind two passages in Luke. The other is the prophetic emphasis on God's sheer generosity, meting out to men more mercy than they deserve, a kind of divine example of "the second mile." In the theistic framework of Jesus and his contemporaries such theology and theodicy is to be expected.

Another indirect way of adding to the actual data of the Gospels is to make logical deductions of our own about a future life from other features of their story. We can believe that Jesus' ethical teaching shows what we should call the conservation of values, the sacredness of individual personality. There are passages where Jesus seems to predate into this life the eschatology of the future, and not merely to make this life determinative for that future. Thus continuity does occur, but in the reverse direction. Scholars are not agreed as to how far proleptic or "realized" eschatology is implied in Jesus' words. From the early days of the church some have understood that foretastes or intimations of the life to come were to be found in the character and historic career of Jesus, and then and now in the life here on earth of his followers. The more it is possible to expect and recognize in the present the ideal aspects of the life of the future the less important does the prospect of later immortality become. Perfectionism as a present philosophy has usually diverted attention from the future, while emphasis upon moral and spiritual limitations of mankind and ourselves here and now have kindled that hope by sheer contrast. Men will differ as to how far the teaching of Jesus aligns itself with the sturdy expectation that men can and will hear and obey his words, and by obedience in this life will approximate his standards and will merit the future rewards. If Christianity has added little of value to the world's conception of a future life, it has rather offered a partial equivalent in our life here.

The Wordsworthian phrase "intimations of immortality" is not only a polysyllabic tongue-twister, but also each word is too easily confused, the first with "imitations," as in one edition of Dowden's introduction to the poet's works, the second with "immorality." The phrase is further only partly appropriate for the thought of Jesus. For him the alternatives were continuous living here until the *parousia* and into whatever is in store for men thereafter or else death followed after an interval of unspecified length and character by a general and/or individual experience of being raised from among the dead. In no strict sense is either of these what we usually mean by immortality.

On the other hand, "intimation" is not a bad description of the nature of the Gospel material. According to the dictionary the word means hint, indirect or obscure allusion or suggestion. This is precisely what the Gospels do give us.

What is more, they indicate the context of the references. They are not speculative but practical. They are associated with Jesus' conversations on conduct. To Jesus and his Jewish contemporaries under the Law the urgent problem was not what to believe but what to do. This was the predicament of man to which he addressed himself. He was for his day and outlook a true existentialist.

The outlook was, however, conditioned. Jesus believed in a God who worked miracles and rewarded righteousness. Any future life, like every present life, is the individual work of God. Man as man is not inherently immortal, nor indeed is any part of him. His body and soul both come into being and they both can go out of being and can both come back into being.

Overshadowing any interest in what would befall his hearers if they should die before the *parousia,* and what would happen or had happened to many generations of men who had died was the expectation of what would overtake the living. At least that appears to be the perspective of Jesus in the Synoptic Gospels. In John's Gospel this is not so clearly the case. Instead of the many who will not taste of death, we have there Lazarus of Bethany who at least did die and was brought back to life and only the possibility that one unnamed disciple unlike Peter might perhaps tarry until the Lord comes.

The expectation of living on until the *parousia* may be the real reason why the Gospels say so little of resurrection. It excludes also the usual idea of immortality as following death. In other words, one may say that eschatology of this sort replaces the need for much concern in the subject appropriate to this lecture, when defined as after death.

I am no expert on the Qumran texts but I do know that they too are heavily surcharged with vivid eschatological pictures, and yet so far as I can tell the published documents have little or no clear reference either to immortality or to resurrection from the dead. It ought not to be attributed to the texts just because Josephus includes in Essene eschatology the immortality of the soul as he does in Pharisaic belief and Hippolytus attributes to the Essenes' faith also resurrection of the body.[14] Perhaps the Qumran documents illustrate how attention when concentrated on apocalyptic hope may leave out as relatively unimportant the question what happens to those who *do* die. I have assumed that the subject of this lecture calls for the latter question. Perhaps I am wrong. In that case immortality should have been construed as including the whole synoptic eschatology and should not have been limited to such passages as imply actual death. The line is confessedly not always clear. But except to modern millennarians the answer of Jesus about those who taste of death would be of more interest than about those who literally will never die. Certainly the first would be at most an intimation of the second.

[14] The material is of course extensive. I refer only to two essays. For the literary sources on the Essenes see Morton Smith, *Hebrew Union College Annual* 29 (1958), pp. 273–313; for the absence thus far of convincing evidence of resurrection belief from Qumran see the unpublished thesis of George W. Buchanan, Drew University, 1959, *The Eschatological Expectations of the Qumran Community*, Chapter 5, note 4. Cf. H. Ringgren, *The Faith of Qumran* (Eng. transl., 1963), pp. 148–51.